ODD JOBS

ODD JOBS

101 Ways to Make an Extra Buck

Abigail R. Gehring

Skyhorse Publishing

www.skyhorsepublishing.com

All interior photos and art, excepting author photo, courtesy of
www.istockphoto.com

10   9   8   7   6   5   4   3   2   1

ISBN-10: 1-60239-033-9 (paperback)
ISBN-13: 978-1-60239-033-1 (paperback)

The Library of Congress Cataloging in Publication Data
        Gehring, Abigail R.
        Odd jobs : 101 ways to make an extra buck / Abigail R. Gehring.
             p.   cm.
        ISBN-13: 978-1-60239-033-1 (pbk. : alk. paper)
        ISBN-10: 1-60239-033-9 (pbk. : alk. paper)
        1. Part-time employment.   2. Occupations.   3. Job descriptions.
    I. Title.

    HD5110.G44   2007
    650.14—dc22   2006102870

Printed in the United States of America

*To my family, for showing me that
variety is the spice of life,
and to Tim, for all you are and do.*

Many thanks to Tony Lyons for my best job yet.

The world is full of willing people, some willing to work, the rest willing to let them.

—Robert Frost

CONTENTS

Chapter Seven: The Oddest of the Odd:
Category-Defying Jobs 189

INTRODUCTION

I grew up in the one-stoplight town of Wilmington, Vermont, where my father was the "Hot Dog Man." Tucking away his master's degree in horticulture and experience as a middle school math teacher, he bought a rusting metal pushcart from a man named Buzz and set up in the True Value parking lot. He worked for twenty-five years, earning enough to put four kids through college and a reputation for his chilidogs that spread down to the Carolinas. I began as "Soda Girl" when I was about five, diving headfirst into the blanket-lined, ice-filled plastic trashcan to retrieve Pepsis for thirsty customers.

Before I could even reach the steamer, I told everyone who asked that I wanted to be a writer when I grew up. But even then I wasn't so naïve as to think I'd make a living doing it, at least not for a long, long time. And, unfortunately from an economic perspective, when I wasn't scribbling in my journal I was in ballet class or at music lessons, developing more unmarketable skills with which to enter the wide world of software engineers and stockbrokers. So whether inherited from Dad, or born of necessity, it seems I was destined for a life of odd jobs.

Now, as I adjust to my first-ever nine-to-five office job (an experience not unlike culture shock, after years of "odd jobbing" to pay the rent), I find myself still answering calls to cater a wedding, henna tattoo adolescent girls at a bat mitzvah, or be a beer promo girl for a night. There's an excitement in doing something totally different, in meeting people I'd never encounter otherwise, and, of course, the draw to make a few extra bucks.

Yes, there is a sense of security in having a "regular" job that one doesn't get when she takes the freelance route. Health insurance is often sacrificed to the gods of flexible scheduling and creative thought, and the term "regular paycheck" is an oxymoron. Even beyond the financial difficulties of a varied work life, there are the social aspects to deal with. How many times have I been asked casually by a new acquaintance, "And what do *you* do?" and had to take an extra ten seconds pretending to chew the bite I've already swallowed to decide how to answer? By that time, the person has lost interest, if she ever actually had any, and is impatiently clicking her wine glass with long red fingernails, glancing over my shoulder for a more promising candidate for conversation. At such moments the best response is to quickly reply that I'm an exotic dancer. Or an Arab terrorist, or a foot model, or anything that will either scare the woman off quickly and painlessly or, with certain curious and risky types, resurrect an otherwise dead conversation.

But the advantages of an odd job lifestyle are not to be taken lightly. Usually, you decide when you work and when you take the morning off to sleep, or the week off to go skiing in Vermont. And the variety of people you will meet, places you'll find yourself, and skill sets you'll discover are sure to keep life interesting, if not always easy, safe, or comfortable. Many of the jobs described in this book are ones that I or one of my financially challenged dancer, writer, or musician friends have experienced out of desperation or fascination at various points in the last several years. But odd jobs aren't only for starving artists. Anyone who could use a little extra cash, who wants to add some spice to his normal work routine, or who's ready to murder his boss and jump the next plane to New Zealand, should peruse these pages for inspiration.

LAWS, DISCLAIMERS, AND OTHER IMPORTANT NONSENSE

Most of the jobs in this book are ones that you can get by calling up and applying to an agency or company that does the sort of work you're interested in. For example, there are hundreds of catering or party entertainment businesses out there that are always looking for friendly, responsible, fun people to join their ranks. Working for an established company means you get the cash and the experience without having to worry about the sticky logistics and constant details of running a business. Some of you, however, will realize as you begin to read these pages that you really don't want to work for anybody else. You'd rather not be told what to do or how to do it, and you're pretty sure you could do a better job than the average Joe or Jill entrepreneur out there trying to stake a claim in the capitalist frontier. You could very well be right. It's also possible that the ideas in this book will ignite a bit of inspiration in you, and suddenly you'll have a fabulous idea for a new business that no one else has thought of, or that's not yet represented in your area. If that becomes the case, there are some details that you should be aware of.

Each state—and often each town or even district—has its own rules for zoning (where you're allowed to set up what sorts of businesses), taxes, insurance, busking, licenses, bedtimes . . . just kidding on that last one. But seriously, it's important to find out what the requirements are so you don't end up paying fines or getting sent to the slammer—even if it does offer free room and board, which might be worth more than what you'll make in the first couple of years in business. If you're just working for tips or you're only making a few dollars here and there, there's a pretty good chance you can get by without reporting anything. On the other hand, if you turn your hobby into a legal business, you can deduct expenses on your tax forms, potentially saving yourself a significant chunk of cash. So if you're going to try flying solo, do your research. The following sites will get you started:

- **www.entrepreneur.com** is a wellspring of helpful articles and information for starting and running a business.

- **www.eventuring.org** is the Kauffman Foundation's guide to building innovative companies, with stories, how-tos, and a glossary of terms.

- **www.tannedfeet.com** is almost overwhelming it has so much information for entrepreneurs of all sorts.

- **www.benlore.com**—The Entrepreneur's Mind offers in-depth profiles of successful entrepreneurs and tells the stories of how they got to where they are.

- **http://sethgodin.typepad.com** is the blog of highly successful entrepreneurial guru Seth Godin. Read it for wisdom and inspiration.

- **www.sba.gov/hotlist/license.html** has links to business license information, listed by state.

- **www.irs.org** is the site to visit for a Tax Identification Number.

- **www.business.gov**—You'll want to check this site out for federal and state licenses, tax information, and other resources listed by subject.

- **www.governmentguide.com**—Here you can type your zip code into the "My Personalized Guide" box and then click on "Small Business" to find the regulations for your city or town (although searches for smaller towns may not yield any results).

While we're getting the legal details out of the way, I should let you know that many of the names, locations, or other defining characteristics in the stories in this book have been changed, mostly to protect the reputations of some of my former bosses. The events are real, however—my imagination is good, but I'm not sure it's that good.

Finally, neither my publisher nor I can take any responsibility for the legitimacy, reputation, or content of the Web sites or other resources listed or the companies or authors they represent. And for that matter, I can't promise you that by the time you pick up this book every detail in every job description will be as accurate as it was the day I wrote it. Of course I'll do my best to ensure that only quality sites are included and that all the information offered is correct and up to date, but heaven knows that Cyberspace, the economy, and life move faster than a Riverdancer on speed. So, use some common sense, do a little research, and remember that if you end up with a lousy job, you can't blame me.

Chapter One

THE SERVICE INDUSTRY

Doing What Needs to Get Done

Pedicab Operator

Personal Assistant

Crossing Guard

Dog Walker

Bike Messenger

Model for Artists or Photographers

Yard Work/Landscaping

Escort

Closet "Exorcist"

Christmas Tree Decorator

Windshield Washer

Rent Out a Room

Pedicab/Bicycle Rickshaw

House-Sitter

Gift Wrapper

House Cleaner

Pooper Scooper

Hospice/Elderly Care

Personal Shopper

I've come to believe that each of us has a personal calling that's as unique as a fingerprint—and that the best way to succeed is to discover what you love and then find a way to offer it to others in the form of service . . .

—Oprah Winfrey

BEADY-EYED RODENT

The biggest issue was the ferret. Sure, there were other things about the job that were a little strange. Like the lengths of damp paper towel strewn about the kitchen, draped over the dish drainer, and hanging from cabinet knobs, because Maria instructed us to reuse them for hand drying until they disintegrated. (I really don't know why we couldn't have just put out a regular cloth hand towel.) There was the day that she asked if I had ever repaired a roof, and when I said no, she told me where to find the hammer, and I guessed that meant I had to figure it out. Out the window I went. Or the way she insisted I stand certain ways in her presence—not hunched but not too rigid, and never in the doorway when she was sitting at her desk facing the window, because it created bad energy. Overall, I made out just fine, considering that she asked one of my friends who also assisted her (for a short time) whether she had had forceps used on her at birth. "Because that could explain a lot," she said, sounding almost sympathetic. "You know, like why you're so *slow*."

But, like I said, the ferret was the clincher. It was a vicious, slinky thing, and it ran freely about the house. Heaven forbid if you should open the door and let it sneak out into the suburban New Jersey neighborhood. This was, perhaps, my greatest fear. There would be no catching the little beast, and though I would have secretly rejoiced in its choice to adapt to an alternative lifestyle, away from the confines of a four-walled home where it had to coexist with me, its escape would surely unleash an entirely new fury in Maria. And it would most likely be the end of a job that, despite its oddities, I wished to keep at least until the end of the summer.

Maybe I never really gave the critter a chance. I have to admit that I disliked it from the moment it stared up at me with its rodent eyes as if it were daring me to do something—what, I'm not sure. I thought for a second that perhaps it wanted me to run my fingers lightly across its glossy coat, but apparently I was wrong, because just then it darted under the table.

Which, I learned, was actually a good thing, since a moment later Maria warned, "Careful. He nips a bit sometimes." *A nipping, beady-eyed rodent. What's not to love?*

I was organizing the cupboard under the bathroom sink when we had our first match. I had an enormous package of toilet paper rolls, which were all supposed to fit in the cupboard, despite the fact that it was already full of cleaning solutions, old toothbrushes, a large bottle of peroxide, bags of cotton balls—you know, all the usual under-the-sink stuff. It was a small bathroom, but I sat on the floor with my legs straddled, sorting things out on the linoleum around me—the first step in the consolidation effort. I leaned forward, working quickly (efficiency was the god of that particular household/business) when I felt a sharp pinch on my lower back, in the gap between the top of my jeans and the bottom of my shirt. I flinched and turned around just in time to see a black streak disappear around the corner. "Ferret . . ." I warned (I was never willing to dignify it by using its Christian name). I set back to work, chuckling despite myself. There I was, sprawled out on a bathroom floor, sorting toilet paper and getting my butt bit by a rodent. The second time it wasn't so funny, and the third time he really chomped down; I actually heard a little rodent snicker as it scuttled away. I stood up, ready for action. I couldn't shut the door because I wouldn't fit in there with all the stuff sprawled out, and besides, I had a sneaky suspicion that ferrets could flatten themselves out and squeeze under door cracks. Maybe it was unfounded, but I wasn't taking the risk.

"Where are you, Ferret?" I called in my most syrupy voice. It peeked its head out from behind a flowerpot and the moment of truth was upon me (although I can't now remember what I'd thought I was actually going to do). But apparently I had spoken too loudly. "What? Is he causing trouble again?" Maria came around the corner, speaking in that little kid, gaga googoo voice that I detest under all circumstances. "Yes, a bit," I answered flatly. To my relief she swept it up in her arms and carried it away, mumbling into its fur, "He must be bored.

Are you bored, little fella?" Although generally I don't support killing animals for their fur, I couldn't help thinking at that moment that Ferret would make a lovely muff.

Ferret's greatest weapon was the element of surprise. He had an impressively developed sense of timing for a creature who was basically a floor mop with teeth. One morning Pam was making business phone calls in the office as I pieced together the fourth scrapbook of business-related articles, letters, and photographs. "We have two different addresses for you, and I'd just like to verify which one is correct," I heard Pam saying. I zoned out again, absorbed in chronological sorting, until a loud yelp broke my concentration. It was immediately followed by quick, breathless apologies as Pam swatted madly at her pant legs with her free hand, a bulge moving and squeaking somewhere around her right thigh. She flinched and I knew he was biting hard. Amazingly, after the initial shriek, she managed to remain composed over the phone, shaking her leg violently while trying to write down an address. I should've helped, but all I could do was stare, aghast.

Pam survived without injury, as did the ferret (unfortunately, I thought at the time), but from that day on we kept our legs curled up Indian style on our seats whenever we made calls. I still find myself occasionally tucking up my feet in office situations, and I get edgy when my shirt doesn't come down low enough in back—survival habits formed in extreme situations don't quickly fade.

In this section, you'll find a description of personal assistant positions such as this one, as well as information on dog walkers, pedicab operators, closet "exorcists," gift wrappers, and more.

1. Personal Assistant

<u>What You Do:</u> This will depend entirely on what sort of person you are assisting. Successful writers, artists, or musicians often seek out assistants because they want to focus on their creative endeavors without spending all their time sorting papers, organizing receipts, cleaning the kitchen, etc. Busy professionals of other sorts who work from their home may want help with mailings, phone calls, or research.

<u>What You Get:</u> $12 to $30/hour for average jobs. If you score a position as a celebrity personal assistant, you could make up to $100,000/year.

<u>What It Costs:</u> Nothing, unless you want to put up a few flyers to advertise your services.

<u>What You Need:</u> Flexibility and versatility are the keys to being a great personal assistant. You should be willing and able to call up the phone company and argue an incorrect bill or clean out a basement, or grocery shop for a family—whatever your employer needs done at the moment. If you are naturally an organized person, you will find you are in high demand.

<u>Perks</u>
- Being a personal assistant seldom gets boring, because you are doing something different every time you turn around.

- If you are assisting someone in a field that you are interested in, this can be a great way to make valuable connections.

- It's often the rich and famous who have the cash to spend on assistants, which means you could become an intimate part of a celebrity's life.

Downsides

- If you don't get along well with the person you are assisting, the job will be miserable.

- Organizing another person's life can turn into a full-time-and-then-some position if you are not careful to set boundaries from the start. If you are a dependable, capable person, you will be a prime candidate for an employer to start relying on you, even during your "off" time.

Sites to Check Out

- **www.princetonreview.com/cte/articles/grads/ personalAsst.asp**—Learn why a celebrity personal assistant is considered "one of the best entry-level jobs."

- **www.celebritypersonalassistants.com** is a staffing firm that provides PAs for high profile sports, business, and entertainment professionals.

- **www.personalassistantpro.com**—Resources for the professional personal assistant.

HOW DO YOU GET THE JOB?

The best way to find personal assistant positions is to search general job listings, such as www.craigslist.com. If you want to be a celebrity assistant, you should first get some regular assistant experience, and then try contacting celebrities' secretaries or publicists to find out if an assistant is needed. Alternately, some general employment agencies staff personal assistants (look through your local yellow pages for contact information). Whatever your approach, be prepared with a resume of your skills and job history, a professional and friendly demeanor, and a willing attitude.

2. Crossing Guard

<u>What You Do:</u> Stand at the crosswalk wearing a bright orange vest and holding a stop sign. At appropriate times, motion for traffic to stop so that school-aged children can make their way safely to the other side. There may also be minimal record keeping involved.

<u>What You Get:</u> $7 to $10/hour. Most crossing guards work 2 to 4 hours a day, when school is starting or getting out, and possibly at lunch time if children are allowed to leave the school property.

<u>What It Costs:</u> Nothing

<u>What You Need:</u> Requirements vary by state—you may need a driver's license, a high school education, and/or first aid certification. Even if these aren't required, they will make you more desirable to employers, so if you have them, mention them when you apply. It's also important to have good hearing and eyesight (it's okay if you need glasses—just make sure you wear them).

<u>Perks</u>
• You may find yourself bonding with the kids and becoming an important part of the community, especially if you're working in a smaller town. One California crossing guard regularly receives cookies, banana bread, and other gifts from admiring children or their parents.

Downsides
• Occasionally drivers decide you're not a real cop and therefore they don't have to stop, even though you're standing in the middle of the road with a stop sign. Many guards quit after just a few days, unwilling to risk the potential of getting mowed down by impatient motorists.

Site to Check Out
• **www.saferoutesinfo.org/guide/crossing_guard/ index.cfm**—Everything you'd ever need to know about being a crossing guard—and then some.

• **www.careerbuilder.com** is a good search site for crossing guard jobs.

• **www.nationjob.com** offers more job listings.

HOW DO YOU GET THE JOB?

Many crossing guard job openings for public schools are listed on city Web sites, as the positions are often paid for by local taxes. If you're interested in working at a private school, you should contact the school directly to inquire.

3. Dog Walker

What You Do: Take someone's dog for a walk, clean up after it does its thing, and return it safely to its owner. Many busy pet owners simply do not have time to give their dogs the exercise they need, so they are willing to pay pretty good chunks of change to have someone do it for them.

What You Get: Part-time dog walkers in New York City make around $200 to $550/week. Sometimes weekend shifts pay more.

What It Costs: Nothing, if you go through an established company. If you want to start your own business, you will need to buy special licenses, insurance, etc., which can be pricey. I recommend trying it out through an existing company first, if there is one in your area. Learn everything you can about the business, and then, if you're still into it, begin researching particular laws for your state.

What You Need: Some companies require you to have a college degree, pet experience, and undergo background checks. Others just require you to be a dog lover—or at least to be really good at pretending you are.

Perks
• Exercise while you work!

• You'll really get to know the walking routes in your area.

Downsides
• You have to be out there, rain or shine, sizzling hot or icy cold.

• Not every dog is a cute, sweet, friendly Toto.

Sites to Check Out
• **www.petsitusa.com**—Links to pet services all over the United States

- **www.prodogwalker.com**—The Professional Dog Walkers Association International site has links to mostly Canadian resources, but it has some useful general information on dog walking as well.

- **www.findadogwalker.com**—You can post an ad here.

4. Bike Messenger

<u>What You Do:</u> Carry and deliver letters and packages around an urban area, via bicycle. The demand for bike messengers has gone down over the last few decades, as fax machines and modems have enabled even speedier written communication. However, pay has gone up, and when there is a need for hand deliveries, bikes are still faster than walking or driving in a traffic-laden locale. Messengers are particularly popular in Beijing and Buenos Aires.

<u>What You Get:</u> Pay is generally based on a commission of $5 to $15 a delivery, equaling about $300/week if you have steady work.

<u>What It Costs:</u> You will need a bicycle and a bag to carry packages in (one with a single strap that goes diagonally across your chest is convenient as it slides easily from front to back without having to remove it), both of which you can get for under $200. Radio systems, if used, are generally provided by the service you work for. And please invest in a helmet, for your mother's sake.

<u>What You Need:</u> Pedaling around a city all day can

be taxing on the body and the nerves. Be sure you're ready for that challenge before you sign on.

Perks

- Bike messengers often think of their job as a sport. Whether work or play, you will definitely get some solid exercise.

- Many cities have bike messenger associations that organize races and celebrations for the annual Messenger Appreciation Day (October 9).

Downsides

- For many, the job loses its appeal the first really windy, rainy, or snowy day.

- As a rule, motorists don't give cyclists much respect, which means you'll really have to keep your wits about you to avoid becoming the inside of a taxi sandwich.

Sites to Check Out

- **www.messengers.org**—The International Federation of Bike Messenger Associations, with links to messenger companies and associations worldwide.

- **www.messmedia.org**—The Messenger Institute for Media Accuracy offers interesting articles, useful tips such as how to choose a good messenger bag, and a downloadable version of the Messenger Industry Handbook.

5. Model for Artists or Photographers

<u>What You Do:</u> Sit, stand, or pose while clothed, nude, or in costume. Art/photography classes always need models, and professional artists often want someone to practice on.

<u>What You Get:</u> $15 to $50/hour. Maybe more if the artwork will be sold or used for advertising. Sittings are generally two to five hours.

<u>What It Costs:</u> Nothing.

<u>What You Need:</u> This is probably the only type of modeling where it doesn't matter what you look like. However, it is helpful if you can sit still, especially for artists working on portraiture. Confidence and creativity in choosing poses will make you a favorite.

<u>Perks</u>
• You'll probably never make money doing less physically or mentally. Most of the time you just sit there. You can think about anything you want and generally pose however you want. I used to practice meditating, but I could never quite separate myself from the sea of heads bobbing up and down as the students shifted their gaze between me and their easels.

Downsides

- Holding one position for an hour or more is harder than you think, even if you get regular breaks. Your nose starts to twitch inexplicably, you notice a throbbing pulse in your ankle you never knew existed before, your eyes start to water . . . A friend was modeling nude for a college freshman art class, knees bent and slightly overlapping as she lay on her side. The pose was a long one, and when she finally got up her legs immediately crumpled under her, limp as soggy spaghetti. What was worse, she decided to pretend it was intentional. So there she sat, stark naked in front of a bunch of snickering students, stretching and yawning as if crashing to the floor was all part of the routine.

- Sometimes it's hard to discern whether the employer is reputable, but it's important to find out, especially if it's going to be just you and the artist alone in a studio. Some artists really do work out of their homes, but if he tells you "Come on over to my apartment and maybe I can, like, take a few shots or something," think twice about what he means by "or something." Find out if there will be other people at the studio, and be clear ahead of time whether you will be modeling clothed or nude.

Sites to Check Out

- **http://figuredrawing.meetup.com** is a networking resource for figure drawers and models.

- **www.wikihow.com/Be-a-Nude-Art-Model** has some useful tips and advice.

- **www.photolinks.com/Photography_Models.html** has links to photography modeling sites.

HOW DO YOU GET THE JOB?

- Call local colleges to see if they offer art classes that may need models.
- Check with community centers and hang flyers to advertise your services.

6. Yard Work/Landscaping

<u>What You Do:</u> Weed, plant, prune, dig, mow, rake, shovel . . . anything to make the land more beautiful and functional.

<u>What You Get:</u> $10 to $30/hour

<u>What It Costs:</u> Nothing, if you work for an already established company (which I recommend if you are new to the business). If you do want to start off on your own, costs can be anywhere from the price of a shovel ($20) to the cost of a lawnmower, rotor tiller, shovels, buckets, a truck to haul it all around in, a business license, and insurance. (If you don't need a loan to buy all that, you probably don't need the job, either).

<u>What You Need:</u> In some states if you are going to advertise yourself as a "landscape contractor," you need to be licensed, which involves taking a comprehensive written test and costs around $75 ("landscape architect" licenses cost more and require extensive professional experience in addition). However, nobody's going to ask for a certificate when you offer to shovel his or her driveway in the middle of a snowstorm. If you want to get more involved (building stonewalls, transplanting shrubs, designing Chinese gardens) but you're not familiar with this sort of technical and artistic manual labor, you can learn a lot by working under the guidance of an experienced landscaper.

<u>Perks</u>
- You get to be outside, work on your tan, and bulk up those arm muscles.

- You'll be everyone's best friend when a blizzard hits.

- If you're just doing casual yard work on your own or with a buddy, you can set your own hours and ask whatever you want for pay. You'll know your price is too high if you don't get any business.

<u>Downsides</u>
- Weather can put a damper (quite literally) on work plans.

- All the bending over and lifting can be rough on your back, and kneeling in the dirt for too long will leave your knees stiff and sore.

Sites to Check Out

- **www.yardworkusa.com** includes useful articles and links to yard work businesses across the country.

- **www.lawncareforum.com**—Read and join discussions on all aspects of the landscaping world.

- **www.landscapejobs.com** has an extensive listing of jobs by state and category. You can also post your resume (for a fee) or check out others if you are looking for someone to team up with.

7. Escort

<u>What You Do:</u> Accompany wealthy men to concerts, the theater, social engagements, and other outings (sorry, gentlemen—although male escorts are sometimes hired to keep a lady company, women are in much greater demand).

<u>What You Get:</u> $200 to $1,000/hour

<u>What It Costs:</u> Nothing

<u>What You Need:</u> You must be highly attractive, confident, well spoken, and be comfortable in both personal and business situations.

Perks
• You will likely be treated to elegant dinners and attend luxurious events.

• You may receive club or gym memberships if your clients enjoy having you accompany them to such places on a regular basis.

Downsides
• If you're thinking this job sounds too good to be true, it's because in most cases it is. Don't be naïve. The majority of men paying $1,000 for an evening are expecting something more than arm candy. However, this does not mean you have to give them what they're looking for . . . no escort agency can legally allow prostitution.

Sites to Check Out
• **www.upscaleescorts.net** is a directory of escort agencies.

• **www.jrn.columbia.edu/studentwork/cns/2002-04-17/171.asp** gives a realistic look at the escort business.

• **www.firstamendment.com/online_escorts.php** is an interesting article addressing the legal issues surrounding escort agencies.

8. Closet "Exorcist"

<u>What You Do:</u> Go to an individual's home and help him or her ream out and organize the closets. For wardrobes, you will work with the client to decide which clothes to keep and which to toss or donate to charity. If appropriate, you might suggest a new

hanging organizer or shelving solutions, or you might just take everything out and put it back on the same shelves in a neater fashion.

 <u>What You Get:</u> $25 to $75/hour, mostly depending on how much the folks in your area are willing to pay.

 <u>What It Costs:</u> Nothing, unless you plan to advertise (but word of mouth is often the best way to get a business like this going).

 <u>What You Need:</u> You should have good fashion sense, excellent people skills, be able to work efficiently, and, of course, be an organized thinker.

 <u>Perks</u>
• You might inherit some of the rejects, especially if you offer to "dispose of" your client's unwanted items.

 <u>Downsides</u>
• Coercing a pack rat to get rid of anything can be like pulling shark's teeth (maybe harder). A friend and I partnered up to help a sweet, elderly Vermont woman clean out prior to a move. Suggesting it was time to part with just about anything (including a shoebox full of her deceased dog's fur) instantly inspired a fearsome waterworks display interspersed with long stories and occasional moans or screams.

Sites to Check Out
- **www.onlineorganizing.com**—This site has a lot of useful articles, tips, and answers to frequently asked questions about becoming a professional organizer.

- **www.organizerswebring.com**—You'll find lots of organizational help here.

- **www.thecontainerstore.com**—There are Container Stores throughout the U.S., and they're great for finding shelving and storage solutions.

9. Christmas Tree Decorator

<u>What You Do:</u> Most families look forward to gathering around the tree, reminiscing over old ornaments, and stringing up the lights and tinsel. But there are plenty of offices, stores, restaurants, hotels, older couples, or individuals living alone that are more than willing to pay to have you do the job for them, especially if they trust you'll do a better job than they could.

<u>What You Get:</u> $25 to $100/hour for a medium-sized tree. To deliver and install a medium-sized tree, you can ask $300 to $400. If you agree to remove and dispose of the tree after the holidays, charge another $50 or so.

<u>What It Costs:</u> This will depend on whether or not the client is supplying the decorations, and, if not, how large the tree is and how elaborately they want it decorated. However, if you will be purchasing the decorations, you should set a budget with the client ahead of time and be sure they are aware they will

be reimbursing you for your purchases. Things of your own you should have include a stepladder or stool ($10 to $25) and clippers/sturdy scissors to trim uneven braches and cut ribbon or wire ($15).

What You Need

• You'll need some artistic vision, enough people skills to determine what your client wants, and enough creativity to figure out how to do it.

Perks

• If you're intrigued at all by this job, it's probably because you enjoy the holidays and decorating. This can be a really fun way to put your creative juices to work.

• This is a great way to earn some extra cash around Christmas, which is when a lot of us become particularly aware of our financial inadequacy.

Downsides

• Pine pitch on everything you wear

• Particularly prickly needles

• Clients who are never satisfied (you get these in any job, though)

Sites to Check Out

• **www.christmascarnivals.com**—There is so much Christmas-related information on this site it's almost overwhelming, but if you only visit one site, this should be the one.

• **www.bronners.com**—This is a year-round Christmas supply store where you can buy standard or specialty decorations individually or in bulk. You'll also find tips, such as how many lights to buy for trees of various sizes.

10. Windshield Washer

<u>What You Do:</u> Walk along heavily trafficked streets, preferably near a stoplight so the cars will be stuck there for a while, and offer to wash dirty windows. You might also try hanging out at a gas station if the attendants will let you. Carry a squeegee and a bucket with water and soap or windshield washing fluid so you can act fast when you have the chance.

<u>What You Get:</u> Most washers work for tips and get about $2 per windshield.

<u>What It Costs:</u> You can get a basic squeegee for under $10 at a discount department store or online and 16 oz. of window cleaning soap for $5.

<u>What You Need:</u> You pretty much have to enjoy rejection to survive at this job. Seriously, if you're an emotional masochist, this is the job for you! Most everybody will turn their eyes away and lock their doors when they see you coming. Only one out of maybe five to ten cars will let you do your job and pay you for it. The thing is, in urban rush hour there's a constant supply of cars, so there's plenty of opportunity for rejection *and* making money. If, in twenty minutes, 100 drivers look at you like you're lower than the bird crap and dead bugs splattered across their windshield (or simply pretend you're invisible), and if you're lucky, you will have scored 10 drivers that let you work; if they each slip you two bucks, that works out to be a dollar a minute. Sixty dollars an hour isn't half bad.

Perks

• Washing car windows is pretty easy work, and no one tells you what to do or how to do it (well, unless the driver starts barking at you to go faster or scrub harder or do it over).

Downsides

• I think the downsides have been pretty well covered: rejection (unless you actually are a masochist, in which case you can pretend this is in the "Perks" section), miserable customers, etc. Also, it stinks when the light turns green and you come within an inch of bonding with the pavement.

Sites to Check Out

• **www.windows101.com** sells all sorts of window washing supplies at reasonable prices.

• **www.detroitsponge.com**—More supplies!

• **www.howtocleananything.com/docs_articles/ hca_article_carwindows.htm**—A window-washing treatise. You'll never have time to be as thorough as these directions recommend, but if you're going to be a professional windshield washer, you should know the facts.

11. Rent Out a Room

<u>What You Do:</u> If you have a spare room in your home, renting it out is a relatively labor-free way to pull in a steady income. I grew up near a ski resort, and our neighbors often rented a room to young people who came to work at the mountain for a season. They made some good friends and some

good money at the same time. It's the least hassle if you can get somebody to stay for several months or a year (assuming it's someone you like), but you can also rent for a night or a week—it will just mean more bed changing, cleaning, and general wear and tear on your home.

<u>What You Get:</u> How much you can charge will depend on your location and the accommodations you are offering. The best way to determine your potential earnings is to look through a newspaper in your area and see what other people are charging. Keep in mind that if your guest will be sharing a bathroom or kitchen with other members of the household, your price will have to be lower than for private apartments.

<u>What It Costs:</u> Nothing, assuming the room is already in decent condition.

<u>What You Need:</u> If you're nice, your guests will be likely to stay longer or recommend your home to their friends. But there will always be people who need a place to stay, even if it means living with a grouch.

<u>Perks</u>
- If you live alone, having someone to share your home with can be really pleasant.

- Besides cleaning before a guest arrives and after they leave, there's not a lot of work involved.

<u>Downsides</u>
• Whenever an extra person comes into your home, your property and belongings are at higher risk, especially if that person's a stranger. It's a good idea to do a background check, and have a tenant who will be staying for a month or longer sign a lease.

• If you don't like your tenant, it will be a bad experience. If you're considering a longer term guest, be sure to meet with him first, talk about expectations, and get a feel for whether he is a person you want to share your home with. If you decide he's not, you better be careful how you reject him or you'll end up with a discrimination lawsuit in your lap.

<u>Sites to Check Out</u>
• **www.room-rents.com**—This site has lots of links that will help you in deciding how much you can charge.

• **www.roommatenation.com**—Post an ad for your room here.

12. Pedicab/Bicycle Rickshaw Operator

<u>What You Do:</u> Transport people around the city in a carriage attached to the back of your bike. Though some drivers choose to work for an established pedicab company, most work independently since pedicab or rickshaw rental fees are generally reasonable.

<u>What You Get:</u> Around $200/day in fees and tips, if you're in a busy metropolitan area. Unlike regular taxis, there is no city-regulated rate for how much pedicab drivers can charge, so it's really up to you.

One Manhattan driver recommends charging a dollar per block, per person (with a maximum of three people in your cab). If you're in a city like Boston, where one-way haphazard street patterns replace blocks, this equates to approximately $10/mile.

<u>What It Costs:</u> To rent a pedicab will cost you roughly $200 a week (or you can purchase one for around $3,000—although, if you happen to find yourself in India, you can pick one up for about a tenth of this price). Some drivers split the cost of rent with a friend, dividing up their shifts, since no one can pedal twenty-four hours a day.

<u>What You Need:</u> A driver's license and the ability to ride a bike. Keep in mind that the bike and carriage will weigh about 150 pounds. Add to that your own weight and a couple of passengers and you could be hauling 800 pounds or more.

<u>Perks</u>
• Great exercise

• You'll be helping out the environment—pedicabs burn calories, not gas, and they leave the air as clean at the end of the day as it was at the start.

• Flexible hours

<u>Downsides</u>
• Severely overweight passengers

• Icy roads

• Other vehicles that cut you off and force you to slam on the breaks when you're straining up a steep hill

Sites to Check Out
- **http://realtraveladventures.com/September 2006/the_rickshaws_of_new_york.htm**—This is a fun and informative article about a first-time pedicab driver in Manhattan.

- **www.ibike.org**—This is the jackpot for bicycle links. With an environmental focus, it's full of articles, worldwide contacts, and links to pedicab companies and manufacturers.

- **www.medialifemagazine.com/news2003/jul03/ jul14/1_mon/news5monday.html**—Learn about pedicab advertising, a potentially lucrative way to supplement your business.

13. House-Sitter

What You Do:
Stay in a home while the residents are away. You act as a security system, the idea being that if it looks like someone is home, thieves or vandals will be less likely to prey on the house. Responsibilities might include picking up the mail, mowing the lawn, buying groceries before the residents return, pet care, and other basic house maintenance.

What You Get: Free rent is the biggest payment. Oftentimes it's the nicest homes that require house-sitters, which means you may get a mansion to yourself for a week, month, or even a year. Sometimes it is appropriate to expect additional pay beyond a fabulous place to crash. Depending on what your responsibilities will be (how many pets you have to care for, how big the yard is, etc.) you could make up to $300 a week.

<u>What It Costs:</u> Nothing

<u>What You Need:</u> You should be responsible and have a good measure of common sense—and not be prone to breaking things. If you don't have previous house-sitting experience, you should have excellent references from landlords or at least from friends and employers.

<u>Perks</u>
• You get to see—and stay in—some pretty sweet places.

• House-sitters are in demand all over the world, pretty much every time of year.

• Most often there is not a lot of work involved in house-sitting. Generally you can live your life as usual, as long as you stay in the house at night and keep up with everyday basic maintenance (put the trash out, water the plants, etc.)

<u>Downsides</u>
• If you make a career out of house-sitting (as many people have managed to do), you will have to be careful not to accumulate many belongings—too much stuff makes house-hopping tricky.

• Though there may not be a lot you have to *do*, you still have a lot of responsibility. If something goes very wrong (e.g. fire, flood, robbery, the dog dies, etc.) there's a good chance you will get blamed, even if it's not really your fault. Of course, this depends on the homeowners and whether they are the type to admit that the house had bad wiring or to insist that you left the stove unit on. You may want to write up some sort of liability contract, especially if you plan to house-sit on a regular basis.

Sites to Check Out

• **www.housecarers.com**—Register as a house-sitter here and post an ad so traveling home-owners can find you. The fee is $35 for 12 months of membership.

• **www.housesitters4u.com** is similar to the idea above, at $10 for 4 months.

• **www.housesitworld.com**—Same deal, only it's free to post an ad for obscure countries—you only have to pay if you want a job in the U.S.A., U.K., Canada, or Australia.

14. Gift Wrapper

<u>What You Do:</u> There are a few ways of organizing a small gift-wrapping business. The easiest is to have people drop off gifts at your home, pick out the paper (if they want to), and return when the presents are ready. A better option, if you have the time and the means, is to offer a pick-up service, where you drive to the peoples' homes, get the gifts, and drop them off when they're all wrapped (you can also charge more for such a service). Alternately, you can ask shop owners if they'd mind if you set up a table inside their store, particularly around the holidays, when shopping activity reaches a frenzy. Then, as people buy their gifts, you can wrap them on the spot. (If the shop owner is initially resistant, offer to give him a portion of the proceeds.) The more heavily trafficked the area, the better you'll do.

<u>What You Get:</u> $3 to $10 per present, depending on the size of the gift. Of course, if it's a recliner or a dishwasher or something, you'll have to charge more. Some gift wrappers make up a price list, while others just wrap for tips. If you do set prices, make sure you'll be getting enough to cover the costs of paper, ribbon, tape, and your time. You can also offer extras, like Christmas ornaments, key chains, small toys, or greeting cards, to attach with ribbon to the gifts for an extra fee.

<u>What It Costs:</u> $40 to $100. Costs will vary according to how elaborate you want to get and how many gifts you estimate you'll be wrapping. For 100 small to medium-sized gifts, expect to pay about $30 for reasonably nice, standard paper; $20 for ribbon; and $10 for tape and scissors. You may also want to buy gift bags, tissue paper, or any of the "extras" mentioned above. Dollar stores and flee markets can be a great resources for inexpensive supplies.

<u>What You Need:</u> With a little practice, anyone can create a beautiful gift, but creativity, efficiency, and an artistic eye will certainly help.

<u>Perks</u>
• Wrapping gifts can be really fun, relatively stress-free, and festive.

<u>Downsides</u>
• Paper cuts

Sites to Check Out

- **www.mommysplace.net/gift_wrapping_ business.html**—Tips and advice for starting a gift-wrapping business.

- **www.profitquests.com/IdeasChristmasGift Wrap.html**—This site is geared toward gift-wrapping as a charity fundraiser, but the same principles apply to personal gain fundraisers!

- **www.superiorgiftwrap.com** sells wholesale gift wrapping supplies.

- **www.mrgiftwrap.com**—More wholesale supplies

15. House Cleaner

What You Do: This one's pretty obvious—you clean houses. Vacuum, scrub, dust, mop, change beds, wash windows . . . you get the idea.

What You Get: $12 to $20/hour if you work through an agency. If you work on your own, you can charge from $50 to $75 for basic cleaning of a three-bedroom, two-bathroom home. Charge more for shampooing rugs, waxing floors, etc.

What It Costs: If you decide to start your own business rather than working for an established company, you'll need all the basic cleaning equipment. You might already have a vacuum (if not, you can get a basic one from Wal-Mart or Target for under $100). You'll also need a bucket (an empty spackle container works well) with glass cleaner, antibacterial spray, a toilet scrubber, rags, paper towels, and sponges.

<u>What You Need:</u> You should be a speedy, thorough, responsible cleaner.

<u>Perks</u>
• You get to see the inside of a lot of great houses. I had no idea how many beautiful homes were tucked in the valleys of southern Vermont until I took a summer cleaning job.

<u>Downsides</u>
• For some employers, you'll never be able to move fast enough, dust thoroughly enough, or check under the couch for dust bunnies enough times.

<u>Sites to Check Out</u>
• **www.house-cleaning-services.com**—Find cleaning services all over the world and links to all kinds of cleaning supply stores.

• **www.house-cleaning-tips.info** has links to dozens of house cleaning–related sites.

16. Pooper Scooper

<u>What You Do:</u> Clean up the doo-doo on neighborhood lawns, using a shovel, dustpan, and a plastic bag. You can dispose of the waste in a few ways: simply chuck the tied-off bag in the client's own trashcan, toss it in a city trashcan (if available), or take it to the landfill. For a more exciting twist, join the circus and follow the elephants around the stage.

<u>What You Get:</u> $7.50 to $15 for a once-a-week visit to a home with one dog. You can charge more for more dogs, and you might consider charging extra for the first visit if there's a lot of residual buildup.

<u>What It Costs:</u> $15 to $30 for a shovel, a "lobby dustpan" (one with a long handle), plastic bags, and gloves. There are fancy gadgets out there for picking up poop, but most of the pros say the old-fashioned way works best.

<u>What You Need:</u> You must be comfortable around animals and their poop. That's about it.

<u>Perks</u>
• The startup costs are so low that you're virtually guaranteed a profit.

• This is a rapidly growing market, believe it or not. More and more pet owners are discovering they simply don't have time to clean up after their pooches.

<u>Downsides</u>
• You're bound to step in it at some point in your pooper scooper career. It happens to the best of them.

<u>Sites to Check Out</u>
• **www.pooper-scooper.com**—This site has domestic and international listings of animal waste disposal companies. It also has some great tips on starting your own business.

- **www.homebiztools.com/ideas/pooper-scooper.htm**—The story of how one man became a professional pooper scooper.

- **www.indulgeyourpet.com/dogs/startpooper-scooper.html** offers more advice for starting a pet waste removal business.

SWIMMING, GOLF CARTS, AND INSANITY

The phone rang, and June leapt from the green metal lawn chair where she had just perched and sprinted back up the lawn to the house. Pink flip-flops swacked against her heels and dyed blonde hair bounced just above her shoulders.

"Hello, Mr. Benson," I said warmly, turning to the elderly man who sat across from me beside the pool. He stared blankly at the space where June had been, leaning forward slightly in his chair, hands gripping the metal armrests. "It's nice to meet you," and because there was still no response, "This is a lovely place you have here." The house was set in a hill, so that the basement opened on one side to the green sloping lawn leading down to the pool and the living room on the first floor looked out to the ocean. Stately flowerpots oozing tiny blue blossoms lined the steps leading from the pool to the basement door.

Suddenly he parted his lips and let out a long, low yell that blasted across the pool water and evaporated in the air beyond. Instinctively, I leaned forward and set a hand lightly on his thigh. "It's okay. June will be right back. She's just gone to answer the phone." His eyes turned toward me briefly, flashing a glimpse of surprise, as if he hadn't realized I was there at all. Then he slumped back in the chair, relaxing his grip on the armrests. Almost immediately his eyelids drooped and his lower jaw went slack. I didn't wake him.

I was ready to drift off myself by the time June returned, the phone stuck down the neckline of her bathing suit and her hands full of towels. "What? Sleeping, Lou? No, no, no. Lou, wake up!" She scratched his scalp vigorously until his eyes jerked open. "You can't let him sleep. He'll never sleep at night if you let him sleep during the day. Lou Benson never took naps. No. Never."

I made a mental note and watched with curiosity as she moved to the front of him. I was searching my mind for a way to politely ask what his condition was. "How old is your father?"

"Lou is my husband," she answered, and I felt heat begin to crawl up my cheeks. "He's eighty-nine."

"Oh, wow!" I said, because it was the only thing I could think of.

"You're comfortable swimming, right?"

I said I was, remembering the ad: "Elderly care. Involves swimming. Part time. $12/hour."

"Lou swims two or three times a day," she said, with a hint of pride. "He loves it. He always loved swimming. Always."

She took both his hands in hers, shaking them a little to get his attention. "Ready, Lou? Time to get up. Ready? One, two, three, UP!" She threw her body weight backwards, attempting to maneuver him into standing position as he sank further into the chair, his eyebrows suddenly hardening into a line.

"Come on, Lou. You can't sit there forever. Let's go." She counted to three again, more slowly this time, her voice getting steadily louder. He looked like he would let his arms be ripped from their sockets before his bottom left that chair.

I got up and stood behind him, sliding my hands under his armpits, ready to lift as June pulled.

"No. Don't help." Her voice was flat but commanding. "He has to do it himself." She took another approach, letting his hands drop back to his lap and kneeling down beside him. "Lou," she said, suddenly quiet and calm, as if she were reasoning with a stubborn child. "You need to get up so you can go swimming. Don't you want to go swimming? It's a beautiful day. Now cooperate, please."

Standing in front of him again, she took his hand loosely, counted, and emphasized the "Up!" with expectancy meant to take the place of the solid yank from previous efforts. Lou looked like he might drift back to sleep. He groaned a little and let his head droop to the side.

"All right, Lou, that's it." Lou widened one eye to stare back at her, apparently recognizing the new determination in her voice. She lifted a bare foot up to the chair, where the metal seat was exposed between his knees. She held his arm, forgetting or choosing not to count, and pulled with everything in her. Lou was standing on his feet before he knew what happened, looking around with a confused alertness, as if he had just woken from a strange dream.

It was that afternoon that I learned how to shave a man's face—in a pool, treading water, while the man fought me as if the razor were a poisonous snake slithering up his neck and cheeks. Oh, and the man was naked—once he got in the pool, fully dressed, Lou was stripped of his shoes, socks, fleece, two T-shirts, and swim trunks (in that order), because . . . well, because that's the way the routine went. And honestly, once I got used to helping him float on his back or paddle back and forth, free as an overgrown baby, it really seemed almost natural—except for the shaving.

"It's just like shaving your legs," June insisted. "You shave your legs, don't you?"

Shaving Lou's face was about as much like shaving my legs as picking a daisy is like hacking down a pine tree with an axe. Every time I sidled up next to him, smearing shaving cream across one side of his face with my left hand, right hand ready with the razor, he'd evade me with a single sweep of the arm that convinced me he must have taken judo in his earlier days. It was quick and forceful without quite being violent, and it pushed me just far enough away that by the time I was close again his cheek was rinsed clean and there was white fluff, like dollops of whipped cream, floating all around us. I tried to be gentle, and then firm, and then I laughed lightly, as if it were all a game. June watched and corrected and eventually did it herself, managing to get his entire face smooth in about three effortless strokes—a skill I would also eventually acquire, with time. I'd also learn to shampoo his hair in the pool (it was easier to bathe him there than get him in and out of the shower), feed him a milkshake with my right hand while steering the old Buick with my left, and swipe chewed up carrots from the space between his gums and cheeks using a spoon handle.

The three of us became friends as the summer wore into fall. I learned that Lou had Alzheimer's and had suffered a stroke that left him unable to speak intelligibly, except for an occasional loud "No!" that bellowed from his lips at inopportune times, as it did when I tried to lift a spoonful of soup to his lips at a local elegant restaurant. And there were a few times when he'd shock us by spewing a whole sentence, out of the blue, and we'd rush to his side like it was a baby's first words. "What was that, Lou? Can you say that again?" But his eyes would show that he'd drifted back to his own private reveries, and no amount of encouragement could get him to speak again.

One of Lou's greatest pleasures was riding in a golf cart. On warm afternoons we'd go to the country club and borrow a cart, June behind the wheel, me in the passenger's seat, and Lou sandwiched between. His eyes would grow wide as the air rushed through his silky gray hair, and often he'd laugh, a hearty "Huh, huh, huh," not unlike one would expect from Santa. When Lou laughed, we all felt as if a weight had been lifted from our shoulders. One day June decided to let him take the wheel. She traded spots with him and I held my breath as well as the seat under me, scanning the greens for potential victims. Lou gripped the wheel like he was born to drive a golf cart, and June slid her foot across his legs to reach the gas pedal. We took off with a jolt and, encouraged by the excitement in Lou's expression, June pressed harder and harder on the gas. We were hurtling down a hill, Lou jerking the wheel from left to right and back again so that I had to wrap my arm around June's back to keep from being slung off the side. All three of us were laughing like maniacal psychos—Lou because he was having the time of his life, June because Lou was happy, and me because that's what I do when I'm terribly nervous and not sure how long I have left to live.

Sometimes I thought Lou was the sanest of our trio. Yes, he swam in the outdoor pool in any and all weather, including January blizzards, when the rest of Connecticut was huddled inside watching all the cancellations stream across the television screen. But he didn't really have any say in the matter. It was June who insisted it was good for him, that it was just like being in a hot tub at a health spa. Maybe she was right—I don't know too many ninety-year-olds as strong as he was. But

I felt terrible every time I aimed the hose at his butt to persuade him to climb the cement steps out of the warm water to his wheelchair, where I'd push him as fast as I could up the icy path, a look of shock frozen on his face as wind and snow swirled around us. When I rolled him inside, both of us shivering and miserable, and June greeted us with, "There, wasn't that fun? Don't you feel better now?" I was pretty sure she was the one touched in the head.

As I later wondered about myself after the day the fourth cordless phone fell in the pool. We always kept a phone with us in case of emergency, and on a semi-regular basis Lou would reach up to the side and drag it into the water before I, or one of the other college students who came to help, could stop him. Or I'd stick it in his jacket pocket so I could have both hands free to guide him down to the pool and forget that it was in there until he, the jacket, and the phone were fully submerged. When the fourth phone died by drowning, June was, understandably, upset. This time it hadn't actually been I who was the guilty party, but when I realized the situation, I was eager to remedy it as quickly and painlessly as possible. First, I tore the phone into several pieces, hoping that if I could get the water out it might revive. However, when the various parts were scattered before me, I could see the moisture still trapped beneath a thin layer of plastic. Since there was not a hairdryer to be found, someone suggested putting it in the microwave. I recognized this as ridiculous immediately—you can't put metal in the microwave. But I thought maybe there was something to the idea of heat, so I popped it in the toaster oven, intending to leave it in there just a few seconds to see if the wetness had evaporated. When I returned, ten minutes later, the phone had begun to ooze into a bright yellow glob. I removed it with a spatula and buried it deep in the garbage can.

There were times when June and I seemed to speak two different languages. One morning, watching the wind blow the snow against the bedroom windowpanes, I suggested, as I had before, that perhaps, for Lou's well-being, we should find an alternate activity to swimming.

"Listen," June said quite calmly, sitting beside Lou and wiping his face with a damp washcloth. "If I were taking care of your baby and you asked me to give it a bath and dry it with sandpaper, would you expect me to do it?"

"No!" I answered, rather horrified at the thought, "I would hope that you wouldn't!"

"No, no. Of course you would want me to do it."

I stared at her, trying to grasp the purpose for this conversation, since having a child was about the furthest thing from my mind. "June, do you feel like I'm not treating Lou the way you've asked me to?"

"No!" she replied adamantly, her voice rising in controlled tension. "We're talking about your baby . . . and sandpaper!"

I never did figure out why we had that, or so many other small arguments. Sometimes I simply didn't understand.

Eventually I knew it was time to move on, despite a growing fondness for Lou and the sizable increase in my salary (up to $1000 a week). I wasn't a nurse and I had no intention of becoming one. Lou was growing weaker and he sat down whenever he got tired, regardless of whether there was a chair in the vicinity or not, meaning that lifting became one of the most prominent parts of my job description. The frigid swims had grown old and, after a fire truck slammed into my car, totaling the vehicle and leaving me whiplashed and shaken, the physical and emotional stress of the job was too much. We parted ways. But I won't soon forget Lou's crazy, hearty laugh, the way he rumbled with pleasure at every bite of food, or our wild rides through the golf course.

17. Hospice/Elderly Care

<u>What You Do:</u> Spend time hanging out with an elderly person, usually in his or her own home. You might play cards for an hour, go grocery shopping, prepare a meal, clean a toilet. Depending on the individual's condition, you may be asked to assist with bathing, dressing, walking, and any number of other tasks. Or you might just be in the room while the person sleeps, in case he or she needs something. Be sure you know what is expected of you before you make any commitments.

<u>What You Get:</u> $9 to $25/hour

<u>What It Costs:</u> Nothing

<u>What You Need:</u> Enjoyment of older people, patience, willingness to listen and possibly to speak loudly. Other requirements may include physical strength, readiness to put up with potentially awkward or gross situations (helping someone use the bathroom or trimming toe nails), and maybe health knowledge and/or related experience.

<u>Perks</u>
- You'll hear some great stories. And have plenty of your own to tell at the end of the day.

- Some live-in situations may offer free room and board.

Downsides
• Work can be draining, emotionally and physically.

• Likely you will not only be dealing with the person you're caring for, but also whoever hires you (generally the elderly person's daughter, wife, husband, etc.), and it can be difficult to meet their expectations. Make sure you get along with who-ever hires you as well as the person you will be caring for. Trust me—it's important.

Sites to Check Out
• **www.eldercare.gov** is full of resources for the elderly and their caregivers.

• **www.ec-online.net** has information and links for those who care for the aging.

• **www.eldercarejobs.com** lists jobs across the U.S. and Canada.

18. Personal Shopper

What You Do: Although shopping is high on the list of America's favorite activities, there are plenty of folks out there who don't have the time, desire, or taste to do their shopping and do it well. Lucky for you, the one thing a lot of those people do have is money, which they will give you to do it for them. It's the Personal Shopper's job to figure out what a client likes and doesn't like; determine his or her budget; and purchase the clothes, décor, beauty items, or whatever else, either with the client (if she's the sort that just wants the moral support and some fashion advice) or to deliver to the client. You can work for an upper crust department store, such as Bloomingdale's, Neiman Marcus, Nordstrom, or Saks Fifth Avenue, or you can develop your own client base and shop wherever you want (or wherever your client wants you to).

<u>What You Get:</u> Full-time shoppers make from $25,000 to $100,000+/year. If you're going solo, how much you charge will depend on how much your clients can pay. It's not uncommon for an experienced Personal Shopper to charge $200 for an initial consultation and close to $100/hour for shopping (purchases, of course, are reimbursed by the client). However, if you're having trouble finding people willing to shell out that kind of cash, bring the price down a bit at first. Once your clients realize how indispensable you are, they'll pay more.

<u>What It Costs:</u> Nothing

<u>What You Need:</u> You must be up on the latest fashions, the newest designers, and the best products. You should know when Gucci is releasing their newest line of purses and always have a list of great gifts to buy for your client's family, friends, or coworkers. Retail and fashion experience are helpful, but if you have a good eye, the ability to override your own taste in order to bring out the best in your client, and a professional, friendly demeanor, you'll do okay.

<u>Perks</u>
• Shop with other people's money!

• If you buy something for your client and she doesn't like it/it doesn't fit right, there's always a chance she'll let you keep it instead of returning it to the store.

- As your client replaces old furniture, clothes, etc. with your purchases, you might get first dibs on the rejects.

Downsides
- You could spend hours searching for the perfect suede shoes with just a bit of a heel and a not-too-pointy toe, only to bring your prize back to the client and be told they're not at all what she wanted. Or worse, that she's changed her mind and wants black strappy spike heels instead ("Oh, sorry. Did I forget to call you?").

- When you're spending all day in a mall, it's tempting to spend all your earnings, too.

Sites to Check Out
- **www.wpersonalshopper.com**—Keep on top of the latest fashions with the help of this site.

- **www.fabjob.com/personalshopper.asp**—This site has a good description of the job, as well as purchasing information for a book on the subject.

TIPS

- As you develop a clientele, create a portfolio of items you've purchased and written testimonials from satisfied (or thrilled, if possible) clients.

- Always look your best when meeting a client. Appearances go a long way in this job.

Chapter Two

MAKING MONEY ONLINE

Virtual Head Hunter

Secondary Marketing Affiliate
Shopping Online
Surveys
Virtual Assistant
Completing Online Offers
Virtual Head Hunter
Selling Books Online
Street Furniture Sales

We've heard that a million monkeys at a million keyboards could produce the complete works of Shakespeare; now, thanks to the Internet, we know that is not true.

—Robert Wilensky

19. Secondary Marketing Affiliate

<u>What You Do:</u> This fancy title is based on the rather obvious principle that a company will waste less time and make more money if they only contact clients who need what they are selling. The way it works is this: companies post their services online with a fee they are willing to pay for referrals. When you hear of a company who needs, for example, 100 laser printers, you look online to find an appropriate merchant. You contact three or four of these merchants, who then contact the company you told them about. If one of them makes the sale, you get paid. This job is called a "secondary marketing affiliate" because the Web site itself is actually the Marketing Affiliate through which you will be working.

<u>What You Get:</u> Some companies pay a percentage of the sales (typically ten percent), others pay a flat fee. If a company makes a sale of $50,000, the Web site gets the 10 percent cut of $5,000, out of which you get 70 percent, which in this case is $3,500.

<u>What It Costs:</u> Nothing

<u>What You Need:</u> This job is all about connections and figuring out who needs what when. If you can do that, you have everything you need to make a lot of money with surprisingly little effort.

<u>Perks</u>
• Connecting a need with a supply and making a significant chunk of cash at the same time—what a deal!

Downsides

• If your friends find out you're the one instigating all those sales calls they're getting all of a sudden . . . well, they might not be so inclined to call you a friend anymore. If you're going to be referring personal contacts, it might be wise to let them know you'll be notifying some potential merchants of their needs.

Sites to Check Out

• **www.innersell.com**—This is one of the leading Web sites specializing in this relatively new concept.

• **www.clickbank.com**—Click on "become an affiliate" to get started.

20. Shopping Online

<u>What You Do:</u> Sign up for a free membership at an online shopping reward site (see below) and do your shopping at one of the stores advertised. Often you can earn by simply opening advertisement e-mails you receive from the membership or by referring friends to the program.

<u>What You Get:</u> For every purchase you make, you will receive an allotted number of points, which can then be redeemed for gift cards at a variety of merchants. Typically 1,500 points ($200 to $400 worth of purchases) can be exchanged for a $10 gift card. Often you will receive around 100 points for getting other people to sign up and a few points for reading e-mails the program sends you.

<u>What It Costs:</u> Nothing

<u>What You Need:</u> Basic understanding of computer usage and the Internet.

<u>Perks</u>
• Most programs have a wide range of participating merchants in nearly every category you can imagine.

• Around the holidays, some programs offer additional incentive programs, increasing the points you earn for each dollar you spend.

<u>Downsides</u>
• It's easy to be misled by the idea that "the more you shop, the more you earn." There's no way around the fact that if you're spending money there will be less of it—not more—in your bank account. However, if you have to buy stuff *anyway* (and we all do, at least once in a while), you might as well get some money back for it.

• It's important to keep track of how many points you earn, as these programs are bound to slip up (probably unintentionally) once in a while and fail to post your correct earnings.

<u>Sites to Check Out</u>
• **www.mypoints.com**—This site has hundreds of participating merchants to shop at and a couple dozen at which you can redeem your points, including Wal-Mart, CVS, Barnes and Noble, and Gap.

- **www.goldpoints.com**—At this site you can shop online or use your membership card to shop at the physical stores. You can also transfer frequent flyer miles or earnings from other select point-earning programs into your account.

- **www.triprewards.com**—This program is the same idea but focused on travel-related purchases (book hotel rooms or shop at participating retailers through your membership and receive gift cards for restaurants, flights, etc.).

21. Surveys

<u>What You Do:</u> Sign up to receive offers to complete surveys on anything from coffee to toothbrushes to cars. If you qualify for the surveys (you're the age, size, color, or whatever that they're looking for), you answer a bunch of questions and hit "submit."

<u>What You Get:</u> Surveys generally pay $3 to $5 each and take 5 to 25 minutes to complete. Some operate on a point system, where you receive a certain number of points per survey, which can then be exchanged for gifts or cash. The more companies you sign up with, the more offers you will receive. By the way, it's a good idea to set up an e-mail account specifically for surveys, as you will start getting a lot of mail all of a sudden.

<u>What It Costs:</u> Nothing. Before I knew better, I paid $30 to sign up for a site promising to increase my money earning potential dramatically. Now I know that there are more than enough surveys you can sign up for without paying a dime.

<u>What You Need:</u> Basic computer and Internet competency . . . and perseverance—there's money to be made, but it takes a while to learn which surveys are worth the time and how to complete them quickly. Most sites require you to be 18 to become a member.

<u>Perks</u>
• You can complete surveys anywhere there's an Internet connection, anytime, day or night.

<u>Downsides</u>
• You'll waste a lot of time beginning surveys, only to be told after several pages of questions that you're not eligible.

<u>Sites to Check Out</u>
These are survey sites with free memberships:
• **www.surveysavvy.com**
• **www.epoll.com**
• **www.mysurvey.com**
• **www.opinionoutpost.com**

22. Virtual Assistant

<u>What You Do:</u> A VA is an administrative assistant that works from home (or wherever you have a computer and an Internet connection). You might do data entry, write proposals, research market trends, send out payroll checks, book flights and hotels, update a Web site, or any number of clerical duties.

<u>What You Get:</u> $20 to $45/hour. If you have special expertise (knowledge of HTML, Web design, or extensive experience in your employer's field) or if you work for an attorney, there is potential to make $100 or more an hour. You might be on call every day or only work a few hours a month, depending on your employer's needs.

<u>What It Costs:</u> Nothing, assuming you already have a computer and basic software applications. If you want to increase your chances of landing a position and learn the ins and outs of the business, there are classes you can take (**www.assistu.com** offers 20 weeks of training for $2,695).

<u>What You Need:</u> You will need to be organized, self-motivated, have good writing skills, and be competent in Microsoft Office. Any additional computer or administrative skills will give you a lead in acquiring and succeeding in a VA job.

Perks
- You will be doing diverse work in the setting of your choice without anyone leaning over your shoulder telling you how it should be done. As long as the work you produce satisfies the employer, it doesn't really matter how you get it done (well . . . try to keep it legal at least—there's no need to go plagiarizing material or stealing software or getting slaves to type up your reports).

Downsides
- Although it's easier to say "no" to a boss when they're hundreds of miles away, if you're good at what you do there will always be people pressuring you to do more for them than you agreed to. If you don't make a clear agreement at the

start and stick to it, you're likely to be getting calls at three in the morning to send an e-mail to a client in Japan.

Sites to Check Out
- **www.ivaa.com**—The International Virtual Assistant Association offers a certificate program, a newsletter, and lots of helpful free information.

- **www.eworkingwomen.com/experts/va.html**— This is a pretty thorough explanation of what a VA is and what you can expect if you become one.

- **www.guru.com** and **www.freeagent.com** have VA job listings.

- **www.msvas.com** is a good place to advertise your services.

23. Completing Online Offers

<u>What You Do:</u> Register to become a member of an online offer Web site and then sign up for subscriptions to products or services (many of which are free trials). If you decide you don't actually want the subscription, you can almost always cancel it within a certain time frame (usually ten days to a month).

<u>What You Get:</u> $2 to $50 an offer (the better paying ones are subscriptions that you have to pay for immediately, but the amount you will get back is greater than the initial investment). Often you can get additional cash for getting other people to sign up.

<u>What It Costs:</u> Nothing

<u>What You Need:</u> Basic computer/Internet competency

<u>Perks</u>
Many of the free trials are cool things you can enjoy for at least a few weeks without paying a cent, like music downloads, online magazines, or dating services.

<u>Downsides</u>
• When you try to explain to your roommate who has just caught you browsing an online dating service that you're just doing it for cash, you can pretty much expect that "yeah, right, loser" look.

• If you don't keep track of your subscriptions and cancel ones you don't wish to keep in a timely manner, you're likely to end up spending a lot more than you make.

• After my roommate started earning money by completing offers, I decided to give it a try. I had quickly accumulated about $100 and was eagerly awaiting my check at the end of the month. When it didn't come, I checked the status of my account to discover I had been rejected by the program because we had both used computers in the same household to complete the offers, which was apparently against the rules. Save yourself some time and read the fine print.

Sites to Check Out
- **www.fusioncash.com**—This is the site that gave me the boot, but if you're careful to follow the rules, you can make some good money really easily.

- **www.treasuretrooper.com** operates on basically the same principals.

- **www.topsitereviews.info**—If you're not sure if a Web site similar to one of the above is legitimate, visit this site and see if it's on the list of recommended links.

24. Virtual Head Hunter

<u>What You Do:</u> Here's how it works. Companies looking for a new employee post an ad on a Web site with a reward for how much they are willing to pay if you can find someone for the job. Then, you see a listing, for example, for a senior sales executive with a reward of $5,000. You happen to have four friends who are currently employed in that field but aren't psyched about their jobs. You refer them, one of them reads the ad, decides to apply, and is offered the position. He gets a new job and you get $4,500 (generally about 10 percent goes to the Web site to cover their costs). If you recommend a friend who then recommends another friend, who gets the job, the reward is divided up so everyone gets a chunk of the dough.

<u>What You Get:</u> Rewards range from $250 to $10,000.

<u>What It Costs:</u> Nothing

<u>What You Need:</u> You'll certainly be more successful if you know plenty of people in the fields most frequently represented on these sites (marketing, advertising, Web site development, and software engineers or architects are particularly popular). Keep in mind that the people you recommend must be already employed and be willing, with the right incentives, to switch to a new job.

<u>Perks</u>
• Referring friends requires only a couple of minutes and it has the potential to benefit everyone involved.

<u>Downsides</u>
• Unless you're the king or queen of connections, you're not likely to score very many times. However, get one friend hired and you've already made a nice addition to your bank account.

<u>Sites to Check Out</u>
Below are two Web sites to get you going.
• **www.jobthread.com** specializes in small to medium-sized businesses and organizations.

• **www.h3.com**

25. Selling Books Online

<u>What You Do:</u> Collect and sell used books online. You can set up your own site, but you might want to start out selling through eBay, www.amazon.com, or one of the other many online book retailers. You

may want to take digital photos of the cover and some inside pages to show potential buyers what condition the book is in. When someone wants to buy one of your books, you have to package and ship it in a timely manner.

<u>What You Get:</u> This will depend on the books you are selling—how rare they are, what condition they're in, and how many you're posting.

<u>What It Costs:</u> Again, this will depend. Look for books at flea markets, thrift stores, and auctions. Keep your eyes open—a friend of mine found one of the first editions of *Jane Eyre* in a cardboard giveaway box on the street.

<u>What You Need:</u> Basic computer literacy. Some knowledge of literature and book appraisal is useful, but these are things you can learn as you go along.

Perks
• Selling books online, especially as a small side business, doesn't take much effort. And no matter what people say about online books replacing the printed word, I'm convinced there will always be enough people who love the feel of a book in their hands to keep the book industry as we know it alive.

Downsides
• If you travel frequently for extended periods, you will need to have someone else package and ship the books when they're ordered (unless you plan to lug your whole collection with you). Buyers

don't like to wait three weeks while you gallivant about. When they order a book, they want it in their hands ASAP.

<u>Sites to Check Out</u>
- **www.auctionbytes.com/cab/abu/y201/m06/ abu0039/s05**—This is an excellent article on how to sell books profitably online. Keep in mind, however, that it doesn't cost much, if anything, to post a book online, so if you have the time, virtually any book is worth posting—you'll be surprised at some of the ugly, old, boring books that sell.

- **www.ebay.com**—You can sell pretty much anything—and definitely books—on eBay.

26. Street Furniture Sales

<u>What You Do:</u> Peruse local streets on trash days, collect discarded furniture (or rugs, dishes, or anything else salvageable), and sell it online. You'd be amazed at some of the things people throw out. I've practically furnished a whole apartment with finds from the streets of New York City, including a bed, bookshelf, table, multiple chairs, rugs, and a great set of dishes. Sometimes things need a little cleaning or repair to make them resalable, but other times you can just tote them home, take a few photos with a digital camera, and post them on eBay.

<u>What You Get:</u> This depends on what you find. If you score a beautiful antique dresser that lots of potential buyers really want, the auction system will serve you well. But even if you only get a few

bucks for an old stool, it's almost one hundred percent profit (minus the cost to post an item online), and that's a few bucks to buy breakfast, or ride the bus, or get a little more than half a Starbuck's latte.

<u>What It Costs:</u> It is helpful to have some sort of large vehicle to collect your finds with, but I managed to get most of my furniture home in a tiny two-door Hyundai hatchback. It's amazing how far a little ingenuity and a dash of brute strength will go. Keep in mind that if you're going to make this into a regular business, you'll need a place to store your finds, too. Rates vary for self-storage units (depending on your location) from about $40 to $200/month for a 5 × 10-foot space. Finally, eBay (and most other online stores) charge a small fee to post your items, but it's seldom more than a few dollars.

<u>What You Need:</u> It will help if you are able bodied enough to lift and move things with relative ease.

<u>Perks</u>
• If kept to a small scale, this is a job you can do totally on your own time. The only thing you have to be regular about is sending or delivering items promptly when they are bought (or you can specify that you operate on a "pickup only" basis—meaning customers must come get whatever they buy from you, but this will significantly limit your sales potential).

• You can continually redo the décor of your home on a regular basis, selling old furniture as you swap it for new and exciting finds.

Downsides
• The success of this job depends greatly on your location. If you live in Hickville, Wyoming, you're not going to find great pieces regularly, whereas there are endless treasures to be found on Manhattan's Upper East Side.

Sites to Check Out
• **www.eBay.com**—The best place to sell your stuff

• **www.moving.com**—Use this site to locate storage facilities near you.

• **www.craigslist.com**—Check out the "free" and "furniture" sections for both acquisitions and sales.

Chapter Three

ENTERTAINMENT AND CULINARY PURSUITS

Renaissance Fairs

Lipstick Reading

Mascot

Renaissance Fairs

Henna/Temporary Tattoos

Dance Host

Human Statue

Face Painting

Balloon Twisting

Santa or Mrs. Claus

Motivational Dancer

Playing a Character

Treasure Hunt Coordinator

Cater Waiter

Ice Cream Taster

Scenic Caterer

Dishwasher

Barista

Fast Food Worker

Gustatory Athlete

Hot Dog Vendor

*If more of us valued food and cheer and song
above hoarded gold, it would be a merrier world.*

—J. R. R. Tolkien

LESSONS FROM LIPSTICK

"I'm here for the Peterson party, please?" My legs wobbled under me as I raced in the direction the valet pointed, having been sitting in the car for heaven knows how long. I had left myself two extra hours to get to Long Island from New Jersey, and still I was late. *Typical*, I thought. It was my first lipstick reading job, and as I passed row upon row of Mercedes and BMWs, I began to form an image of what the hostess would look like when I stumbled in to the birthday party fifteen minutes late. She would stare down at me from where she perched high up on her stiletto heels, hair billowing in enormous waves as she aimed a long, spindly manicured finger at me and pinched her too red lips together in a tight thin line. I had seen it before at ritzy country clubs—that perfect withering combination of disgust and condescension.

I hurried through halls dripping with chandeliers and scattered with enormous bouquets, soliciting men in formal suits for directions as I went. When I found the Peterson party, I didn't even know it. There were only a few women, smiling and chatting as they directed chairs to be moved or a tablecloth changed. "Excuse me." I stopped one of the women. "I'm looking for the Peterson party. Do you happen to know . . . ?"

"Oh, good!" She interrupted. "You must be the . . . the . . . now, what was it you were going to do?"

"I'm the lipstick reader."

"Right! Excellent! Can I get you something to drink? What do you need—a table?" She was already moving away to find me a place to set up. She was tall with high heels and big hair, but her lips were a gentle shade of coral and there was no accusatory pointing. I was beginning to wonder if maybe my instructions were wrong and I was, in fact, on time. I decided to at least pretend this was the case.

I sat down on the chair the bartender had brought over for me and began pulling things out of my bag. My legs had stopped shaking, but my hands were trembling instead, which was worse now that they were in the spotlight as I handled the small white cards. The fact was I didn't know what the heck I was doing. For training, my boss had thrust a stack of papers at me and told me to read it before the gig. When I sat down to look through them, I discovered that large sections of the text were missing and what was left was so out of order that I gave up. The concept of guessing a woman's personality based on her appearance had seemed like common sense, but as I lined up the lipstick on the table, I wished I had tried a little harder to sort out those instructions.

I put on the leopard print coat I had been instructed to wear by my eccentric Jewish lesbian boss. I looked at the red beret she had insisted was "Oh! Perfect!" and shoved it back in the bag. I was feeling self-conscious enough without sticking a flaming red felt cap on my head.

My first customer was a woman whom I guessed was about thirty-five, with blonde shoulder-length hair. Her lips were already glossy pink and she refused a new coat of lipstick, so there was nothing to do but to begin my analysis. She was smiling as she handed me the card, now decorated with a voluptuous pink print traced with white spidery lines. I studied it carefully for too long, buying time, searching for words that were both vague and insightful. "You're a very warm person," I ventured finally, quickly glancing up to catch her reaction. Her eyes brightened and the two ladies hovering behind began to nod to each other, raising their eyebrows expectantly. Encouraged, I continued. "Your friends enjoy spending time with you because of your kind-hearted, open approach to life." *Where did that come from?*

"Yes, yes," the backup women agreed as my customer touched her fingertips lightly to her chest, modestly accepting the flattery. I turned the paper sideways, as if considering it from a new angle, and narrowed my eyes a moment before speaking again. "Because you give so much of yourself, you often realize, when you have a moment to stop and think, that you feel exhausted, isn't that right?"

Her lips parted slightly and she leaned her weight backward in the chair. "How did you know? You can read all that from my lips?"

Instead of answering, I continued, "I suggest you take some time for yourself these next few weeks. Take a bath, get a massage. You need to rejuvenate yourself so you'll have what it takes to help others again in the near future." The friends had grown silent, but as I handed the print back to the woman they began to exclaim, "Wow! She's good! And she can tell all that from her lip print! Who's next?"

This isn't so bad, I decided as the woman got up and another took her place.

The next lady had not been one of the primary commentators during my last "reading." I had vaguely noticed her off to the side, as if she were amused by the scene but didn't want to appear as part of it. She had only sat down at the other women's insistence, and her eyes darted skepticism. She had a neutral lipstick, her suit jacket was a dull gray, and her eyes were a deep brown, matching her long hair. I almost began my analysis before taking the paper from her, I was so confident I had her pinned, but I caught myself and gave it a reasonable study before speaking. "You are very fastidious—you can't stand to see a project done less than perfectly . . ." She snorted and there were no approving nods from the other women.

"That's not me at all," she replied flatly and, I thought, almost victoriously. There was no way to stop the blood from rising in my cheeks.

"Really? Oh, well, you know, these lines are vague . . ." I turned it this way and that, holding it closer to my face. "Generally it takes a darker shade of lipstick to make a suitable print. Would you kiss this again for me?"

Things improved again after that. I managed to somewhat salvage the reading I had just butchered by reversing what I had said, since I was clearly so wrong the first time ("You have a carefree spirit," etc.). For the next woman, I started off with less specific, safer assessments, like "You like to socialize, but you also need time alone." I told her that she was introspective and guessed that she liked to journal, based on the way her eyes seemed calm but reserved, and on her simple mauve sweater.

"Yes!" she answered, suddenly excited. "In fact, I was just telling my husband last night that I'd like to write a book."

"Mm hm," I responded, as if I had known for sure that she would say that. "This is a good time for you to focus on your writing and see where it takes you. I sense that there are people who will come into your life to encourage you and help you in that area if you devote a little time to it each day."

"That's so amazing!" She turned to the hovering women. "Can you believe I was just telling my husband that last night? I'm going to do it." She started to get up, so determined I wondered if she was leaving the party right then and there to go write.

Another woman left convinced it was time to go back to teaching at a Manhattan school, all because I ventured that she was a very sharp thinker and had a lot to share with others—based mostly on the way she annunciated when I asked her if she was enjoying the party.

The hour flew by. People were asking me for my number because their daughter/sister/mother was having a shower/birthday/engagement party and lipstick reading would be just the thing to liven it up! Even the bartender wouldn't let me leave until I'd read his lips. When I said goodbye to the hostess and walked out past the chandeliers, the doorman, and the rows of Mercedes back to my little hatchback Hyundai, I took off my leopard print jacket, laughing to myself. I had never expected to be so believable—what else could I pull off with a funky jacket and a confident smile?

In this section you will find all things entertainment-related, beginning with "Lipstick Reading" and including "Motivational Dancer" and "Santa or Mrs. Claus." Once you've passed "Treasure Hunt Coordinator," you'll discover the culinary pursuits.

27. Lipstick Reading

<u>What You Do:</u> This is a rather unusual form of party entertainment, popular at middle-aged birthday parties, bridal showers, and charity events. First, a little background: lipstick reading is a descendant of physiognomy, the science of discerning a person's character by careful observation of their facial features. It's been a part of Chinese medicine for centuries. But most lipstick readers are far from being doctors. Basically, you paint lipstick onto a woman's lips (you can skip this part if she already has enough on) and ask her to kiss a piece of paper. You study the lipstick print on the paper for a while, hum and hah, and tell her something about her personality, and, if you feel so inclined, about her future. Believe me, you can tell a lot about a person just by looking at the way she dresses, her hairstyle, her posture, and listening to the way she speaks.

<u>What You Get:</u> $25 to $50/hour

<u>What It Costs:</u> $30 for lipstick (lip gloss palettes work well because they come with multiple colors and a brush).

<u>What You Need:</u> Creativity and at least a little intuition.

<u>Perks</u>
• This is certainly not a labor-intensive job.

• It's creative, quirky, and playful

• If you're good, people will think you're a genius!

Downsides

It feels a little phony sometimes, because, well, it is.

Sites to Check Out

- **www.partypop.com** is a site with links to event planners across the country. However, most people still haven't ever heard of lipstick reading, which means you may have a hard time finding a party planner that is actively seeking lipstick readers (**www.boutrageous.com** is one New York City-based exception). However, if you contact party companies in your area and explain what you can do, you might become the newest sensation in your local entertainment industry!

- **http://face-and-emotion.com/dataface/physiognomy/physiognomy.jsp** and **www.aryabhatt.com/women/women.htm** offer information on physiognomy.

28. Mascot

What You Do: There are many kinds of mascots. You're probably picturing major league baseball mascots like the Baltimore Oriole leaping through the air, doing flips, and generally astounding the audience with feats of skillful agility. You're also probably thinking you'd kill yourself the first hour on the job. But don't forget bank mascots, who just have to hand out flyers, pose for pictures, and try not to faint in their costumes. There are school mascots, who do silly things to make the kids laugh, and promotional mascots, who give out balloons at car dealerships or march in parades. However, if you *are* gifted in the areas of stunts and entertainment, go for the major sports. Some of those furry fellows make serious money.

<u>What You Get:</u> From $20/hour to a six-figure salary (for professional sports teams).

<u>What It Costs:</u> Generally, whoever hires you will provide the costume. But if you want to buy your own for any reason, you'll be spending $400 to $600 or more.

<u>What You Need:</u> Regardless of whom you're representing, your job is to entertain and draw attention. So if you're not into crowds and being in the spotlight, you can turn the page now. You should also be prepared to be hot—and not the sexy kind. Overheating and even fainting is not uncommon for mascots.

<u>Perks</u>
• The potential to have a whole stadium laughing, clapping, and cheering because of you!

• Or at least a bank customer snickering despite himself

<u>Downsides</u>
• As mentioned, costumes are usually hot!

• Serious mascot positions can be risky—Wild Wing of the Anaheim Mighty Ducks was supposed to spring off a trampoline and catapult over a wall of fire. Tragically, his skate got caught in the trampoline and, well . . . roast duck, anyone?

Other mascots have lost parts of fingers, sprained multiple body parts, been taunted and abused by fans of opposing teams, and received numerous blows from stray balls.

Sites to Check Out

• **www.mascots.com**—Street Characters Inc. auditions mascots for high profile jobs.

• **http://ga.emascotcostume.com**—If you're looking for a costume, you'll find lots of links here.

• **www.promascot.com** has job listings for various sorts of mascots across the U.S. and Canada. Just click the "jobs" tab.

29. Renaissance Fairs

What You Do: If you've ever been to a renaissance fair, you've seen the food vendors selling enormous legs of meat; the buxom women hurrying about leaving lipstick marks on the cheeks of unsuspecting men; the men staging sword fights; the girls selling armfuls of flowers; the stable hands leading ponies carrying children in circles around the field . . . festivals sometimes employ up to 5,000 individuals to create an exciting, unique, authentic (sort of) experience for guests. Most festivals have a "job faire" to hire help prior to beginning a season in a particular area. On the job, you will be dressed up in period-specific clothing and be expected to converse with guests in an appropriate dialect, always maintaining the character you are assigned, whether you're taking guests' tickets, manning the rides, or mud wrestling.

<u>What You Get:</u> $7 to $25/hour, or at least a free lunch and discounts on merchandise, depending on the festival and the skill your position requires (e.g., if you're juggling with fire, you'll make more than if you're picking up trash, even though juggling is much more fun . . . that's just the way it goes).

<u>What It Costs:</u> Nothing, although if you are doing a specialty act, such as a magic show, you will be expected to bring your own props.

<u>What You Need:</u> You should be willing and able to ham up the part—this job requires a certain amount of acting, creativity, and willingness to be mocked.

<u>Perks</u>
You'll meet interesting people, get to be outside, and live a fantasy life for at least a couple of days a week.

<u>Downsides</u>
• You may not have much say in what position you get, which could mean cleaning toilets.

<u>Sites to Check Out</u>
• **www.renfaire.com**—This site will help you figure out proper pronunciation, show you how to dress, and direct you to fairs across the country.

• **www.faires.com**—Search for festivals by date, location, or simply view the whole list.

• **www.ehow.com/how_17229_become-part-renaissance.html** has some useful tips on how to break into the renaissance festival world.

30. Henna/Temporary Tattoos

<u>What You Do:</u> Use henna, eyeliner, or non-toxic acrylic paint to create designs on arms, ankles, or shoulders. Temporary tattoos are popular at teenage events, like school-sponsored graduation parties. Recently some beer companies have hired henna artists to liven up their promotional events at bars. Alternately, you can set up a table in a busy park and offer tattoos for tips.

<u>What You Get:</u> $25 to $50/hour, or, if you're just doing it for tips, about $3 to $5 per customer.

<u>What It Costs:</u> You can buy three tubes of henna paste (enough for about 60 small to medium-sized tattoos) for $15. Eyeliner is even cheaper, at about $3 to $5 per pencil or liquid eyeliner. Acrylic paint applied with a medium quality paintbrush is the easiest and lends the best results; at $2 for a bottle large enough to last for hundreds of designs, it's also a darn good deal.

<u>What You Need:</u> You will need some artistic skill, but maybe not as much as you'd think. You can find tattoo designs online for inspiration, and a little practice goes a long way. Henna tattoos last several weeks, so there's a little more at stake than with eyeliner or paint, but traditionally henna designs are simpler—dots and swirls in interesting designs, rather than jumping dolphins or flying dragons.

Perks

• This is a chance to be creative in a fun environment and get paid for it.

• People will think you're cool, especially if you're good at it.

Downsides

• It stinks when you get a fifteen-year-old tough guy who's already got snakes and crosses and tribal designs climbing up and down his arms and he asks for something you know you can't do to save your life (like, for me, praying hands). Those kids are masters at giving you a look that will make you feel like some sort of sorry excuse for cheap entertainment.

• It also stinks when the henna tube gets clogged and you squeeze harder and harder until suddenly a huge blob of paste explodes from the end and ends up oozing down some woman's forearm. (The trick in such a situation is to pretend that that was *exactly* what you meant to do, and somehow turn it into an artful design. Also, you can avoid this problem by bringing a needle to stick in the tip when it starts to feel clogged).

Sites to Check Out

• **www.hennaking.com**—This site has great prices on henna, as well as free designs you can print off for your portfolio.

• **www.tattoospot.com**—Here you'll find lots of pictures of tattoos you can use for inspiration, though many of them are on the complicated side.

• **www.freetattoodesigns.com** has more ideas, with dozens of links to other tattoo-related sites.

31. Dance Host

<u>What You Do:</u> Dance with partygoers who otherwise might not have a partner. It's your job to make people feel comfortable on the dance floor and to make sure anyone who wants to try out their moves has the opportunity to do so. Dance hosts are particularly popular on cruise ships.

<u>What You Get:</u> $25 to $100/hour

<u>What It Costs:</u> Nothing

<u>What You Need:</u> You should be confident, be a competent dancer, and ooze charm. It's helpful to know the basics of ballroom, but not always necessary.

<u>Perks</u>
• You get to attend parties, dance, and probably enjoy the same food the guests do.

• You'll be the star of the party—former wallflowers, this is your chance to shine!

<u>Downsides</u>
• You will not always want to dance with everyone, guaranteed. There are guys out there who apparently think dancing is only fun if it involves ripping the woman's arms out of the sockets, and women who think the more they wiggle the sexier they are (and this is simply not true).

Sites to Check Out
• **www.dancinglist.com/Hosts/Host1.htm** offers a listing of agencies and a place to post your résumé.

32. Human Statue

What You Do: Dress up as the Statue of Liberty, a doll, the Tin Man, or any other inanimate object. Your goal is to make people think you're made of concrete or stone until you shock them by batting an eyelash, cracking a smile, or waving. Ninety-five percent of the time you'll just stand perfectly still on a pedestal. Then, out of the blue (or more specifically, when you get a tip), you change your pose.

What You Get: Most human statues work for tips, so how much they make depends on how heavily trafficked the area is, how good they are, and how generous the passersby feel. However, you might be able to hire yourself out as an entertainer at celebrations or promotional events, in which case you can make $25 to $100 an hour.

What It Costs: Costume prices will vary. If you dress up as a doll, you might be able to wear clothes you already own—a cute plaid skirt, stockings, a blouse, and some rosy blush. However, if you're going to be the Statue of Liberty, you'll need a torch, a cloth to wrap around yourself, a crown, and green body paint (all of which you should be able to get for under $30).

<u>What You Need:</u> It does take a certain amount of skill and practice to stand perfectly still. Good statues don't even blink unless they decide to.

Perks
• Startling people so badly they almost fall over

• Next time someone tells you "Don't just stand there! Do something!" you can confidently reply that you make a living "standing there" and it's perfectly legitimate behavior.

Downsides
• There will always be one jerk who thinks it's great to tickle, poke, or otherwise harass you. If you're dressed as a soldier, this is the point at which you suddenly whip out your sword or gun (fake, of course). If you're a ballerina, you can demonstrate your beautiful kicks, and the Statue of Liberty— well, you'll have to be creative, but I'm sure it wouldn't be the first time a torch has doubled as a weapon of self-defense.

Sites to Check Out
• **www.calmerkarma.org.uk/statues.html**—This U.K. site has some great pictures for inspiration.

• **www.costumes4less.com**—There are some decent costumes on this site for reasonable prices if you can't piece together your own.

33. Face Painting

<u>What You Do:</u> Paint faces at kids parties, at fairs, or at the park.

<u>What You Get:</u> $25 to $50/hour if you work through a party company or agency. If you're doing it just for tips, earnings will vary significantly.

<u>What It Costs:</u> $15 to $20 for a set of face paints from the craft department of your local department store.

<u>What You Need:</u> It's helpful to have basic artistic ability, but how elaborate you get is really up to you. It may take some practice to be able to do a full-face multi-color butterfly design, but you don't have to be an artistic genius to paint three balloons or a pink heart on a kid's cheek.

<u>Perks</u>
• Kids are surprisingly flexible—if a little girl tells you she wants a horse on her forehead, and you know darn well you can't paint a horse for your life, you can usually say, "Oooh, I have an idea! You know what would look really pretty? How about I make you a princess with a bright, beautiful gold star on each cheek!" Chances are, she'll go along with it and never even consider that princesses don't usually have stars on their cheeks.

Downsides
- Sometimes the mom is more intent on getting those cat's whiskers on her child's cheeks than the kid is, which means there are always a few squirming, whimpering children to paint.

Sites to Check Out
- **http://painting.about.com/od/facepainting designs**—Here you'll find face painting designs, tips, photos, and a directory to other helpful Web sites.

- **www.facepaintingdesigns.co.uk**—A British site with wonderful step-by-step instructions for full-face designs.

- **www.facepainting.net** has lots of photos, including some pictures of elaborate body art.

34. Balloon Twisting

What You Do: Twist balloons into interesting animals, hats, or toys. The simplest way to start out is to set your self up in a public park that is well trafficked and work for tips. Sometimes restaurants will let you entertain guests while they're waiting to be seated, too. Alternately, you can work through a party planner or an entertainment company.

What You Get: Expect $3 to $5 per balloon creation in tips. If you're in a great spot (lots of kids with parents willing to spend money on them), you can make a couple hundred bucks or more in a day. If you're being paid by the hour for an agency, you should make $25 to $50/hour.

<u>What It Costs:</u> You can get a cheap electric balloon inflator and a bag of balloons for $10. If you want to make it big in the balloon industry, you might need a better pump, which could cost upwards of $100.

<u>What You Need:</u> You'll have to learn how to twist, but there are Web sites that can teach you that (see below). You should be a nice person, too. Nobody wants a balloon from a grouch or a snob.

<u>Perks</u>
• Flexible hours

• Making cute kids smile

<u>Downsides</u>
• If you're working outside, weather can ruin your best laid money-making plans.

<u>Sites to Check Out</u>
• **www.balloonhq.com**—This site is a veritable balloon treatise. From the technical explanation of why balloons pop to tax information for starting your own ballooning business, you'll find it all.

• **www.balloonanimals.co.uk** is a fun and funky site that will guide you with pictures, simple instructions, and animations.

• **www.lpballoons.com** is a wholesale balloon retailer, if you find yourself doing a lot of twisting and needing some serious supplies.

35. Santa or Mrs. Claus

<u>What You Do:</u> Santas are particularly in demand at malls around Christmas time, but you can also hire yourself out to entertainment agencies, start your own business for private or corporate parties, or partner with a photographer and set up at schools, parks, events, or anywhere where there are children and parents with money. You smile, laugh (practice your ho-ho-hos ahead of time, Santa), and listen to children's requests. It will be more difficult to land jobs as Mrs. Claus, but Santa's better half can make herself a hit by providing baked goods for parties (who can turn down a freshly baked cookie served by a sweet old lady in red?), teaching crafts (e.g. making simple, cute toys), or just being a warm and nostalgic presence.

<u>What You Get:</u> Mall Santas make from $10 to $20/hour. If you hire yourself out privately for parties, you can charge $50 to $100/hour.

<u>What It Costs:</u> Santa suits range from $25 (for simple flannel and polyester designs) to $700 (for the velvet deluxe lines). Mrs. Claus, you may be able to get away with a red dress, white apron, and a bonnet, or buy a costume like your man. If you're doing crafts or baking, you'll need additional supplies.

<u>What You Need:</u> You must look the part. Santa, that means big belly, smiling eyes, and a real beard if you can pull it off. Mrs. Claus, you should be on the plump side, too (though not big like your husband), have gray hair, round glasses, and rosy cheeks. Also, you have to like kids, or else you'll be miser-

able, and nobody wants to hire a miserable Santa. For mall Santas, you'll undergo a background check.

Perks
• Seeing the kids' eyes light up when they really believe they're encountering the wonderful characters their parents have told them stories about.

• Candy canes are usually in good supply.

Downsides
• Screaming kids

• It's very seasonal work, from November through January 1 (or maybe that's a good thing—there's a reason the real Santa retreats to the North Pole for most of the year).

Sites to Check Out
• **www.santaschool.com**—Yes, there really is a school just for training Santas.

• **www.santaforhire.com** hires and contracts out Santas all over the world.

• **http://santasuits.com**—For all your costume needs.

TIPS

• Never "ho-ho-ho" too loudly when kids are close by, unless you intend to frighten them all to tears.

• Only pick up children from under their armpits. You don't want a lawsuit on your hands.

• Be prepared with answers to the tough questions/ requests ("How will you get inside if we don't have a chimney?" "I want my mommy and daddy to love each other again").

36. Motivational Dancer

<u>What You Do:</u> Dance, clap, sing . . . whatever it takes to get the folks at the party grooving out on the floor with you.

<u>What You Get:</u> $30/hour is standard.

<u>What It Costs:</u> Nothing

<u>What You Need:</u> Lots of energy, no inhibition on the dance floor, ability to move to the beat. The level of necessary dancing skill will vary. Some entertainment companies will want to know that you've had formal dance training, others just want you to be the life of the party. Hip-hop experience is a definite plus, as motivational dancers are most often hired for bar/bat mitzvahs, sweet sixteen parties, and other events where teenagers prevail.

<u>Perks</u>
• There's a good chance you'll get a free meal out of the deal. Most hosts feed the entertainment.

• Get paid to work on your moves.

<u>Downsides</u>
• You will be expected to be peppy, often to the point of being obnoxious.

• Heaven knows adolescents can be less than angelic.

<u>Sites to Check Out</u>
- To find a party planner in your area go to **www.partypop.com**. Contact local companies and inquire whether they hire motivational dancers.

- **www.alltimefavorites.com**—If you're thinking of teaming up with a DJ or other entertainers, this site will point you in the right direction.

- **www.partydirectory.com** has more links to entertainment companies across the nation.

37. Playing a Character

<u>What You Do:</u> Dress up as a character—usually a Disney, popular television, or superhero figure, such as Cinderella, Spiderman, Barney, Belle, etc.—and make an appearance at a party. You might be asked to lead kids' games and songs, or you might just wander around and let people take pictures of you with their little ones.

<u>What You Get:</u> $25 to $100/hour if you do it through an agency or party planner, and possibly more if you branch out on your own (but your expenses will be more, too). Most kids' parties last 2 to 5 hours.

<u>What It Costs:</u> Probably nothing—usually the agency will supply the costume and any props. If you're going solo, costumes cost $50 to $150.

<u>What You Need:</u> You should be good with kids, willing to be silly, and able to act in character.

Perks
• Isn't it everyone's dream, deep down, to be a princess or a superhero?

Downsides
• Cookie Monster costumes tend to be really hot.

• Cinderella skirts seem to attract little boys who think they make great tents (yes, I speak from experience).

• Spiderman costumes are basically the equivalent of spandex tights, a muscle shirt, and a dyed rubber glove stretched over your head—or at least they feel that way, from what I gather.

Sites to Check Out
• **www.craigslist.com** often lists party-related jobs under its "Etc." section.

• **www.partypop.com** has links to entertainment companies across the U.S.

38. Treasure Hunt Coordinator

What You Do: Develop treasure/scavenger hunts for birthday parties, bat/bar mitzvahs, bachelorette parties, summer camps, or any group who wants a team-building activity. You'll have to make up clues and hide them, prepare prizes (unless the client provides them), and be present during the hunt to monitor and encourage the participants. You can keep it as simple as fifteen clues hidden around the first floor of the client's home, or make it as elaborate as a citywide, limousine-chauffeured, professionally photographed event.

<u>What You Get:</u> How much you can charge will depend on how extravagant and complicated the hunt is, whether or not you provide prizes (and what they are), and how long it takes to complete the hunt. For a very simplistic hunt with candy for prizes that lasts half an hour (which can still be an exciting experience for kids), you might charge $75. Some companies offer intricate, adventurous, posh hunts in museums, amusement parks, or throughout a wide range of city landmarks, which cost thousands of dollars. If you work for a scavenger hunt business as an employee, you might get $25 to $50 per hour.

<u>What It Costs:</u> Again, there is such a range in types of hunts that it's almost impossible to set a price on necessary supplies. At the low end, a few bags of candy and paper to write the clues on could cost less than ten bucks. On the upper end, the possibilities for spending are endless. Keep in mind that if you're doing anything that could even possibly be dangerous, you'll need to have liability insurance.

<u>What You Need</u>
- A knack for developing clever clues (it's especially cool if you can customize clues to your client and to the environment where the hunt will take place).

- The energy to get a group of people (kids or adults) excited about your hunt.

<u>Sites to Check Out</u>
- **www.drclue.com**—This site and the ones below are companies that are already established in the treasure-hunting world. Whether you want to become an employee of one or start your own business, these are worth a visit.

- **www.watsonadventures.com**

- **www.treasurehuntadventures.com**

A NIGHT AT THE CRICKET CLUB BALL

We set out walking, beginning the gradual ascension up West Way, the three of us looking like a trio of penguin hybrids in matching black pants and white-collared button-down shirts. The sun was sinking slowly, still well above the rows of hedges and rooftops that stretched from either side of Oxford proper. We went quickly anyway, unsure of exactly how far it would be to the King's Arms, where we were scheduled to arrive at six. "It's just straight up that road," Vick—my new boss—had told me. "Where did you say you live?" "80 West Way. Just across from the Co-op," I reminded her. "Oh, right. Brilliant. It's not far at all, then. You'll see it."

It was only my second assignment since being hired by the Botley Catering Company. For the first one, I had found myself, after a seemingly endless bus ride, standing in front of an enormous hardware store. I had thought for sure it was the wrong address, that I had perhaps gotten on the wrong bus altogether, and that no doubt I would lose my job before it had even officially started. Upon further inquiry and exploration I discovered, however, that there was a tiny café tucked in the middle of the rotor tiller section, far beyond the potting soil, light bulbs, drills, and shovels, where a growing mound of dirty plates, teacups, and mixing bowls was awaiting my dish-washing skills.

This assignment was of a very different nature, though. It was the annual Cricket Club Ball, Vick had explained over the phone, and I had felt a quick surge of nervous excitement as she said the words. She asked if I had any friends who might like to work also, as they were particularly short-staffed that weekend, so I had convinced Lauren and Monica, two other American students, to join me.

We had not been walking long before we came to a split in the road. We barely ever walked that direction (away from the city) and none of us had any particularly good reason to go one way over the other. We chose left, because it looked more pop-ulated, and picked up the pace even more, aware of perspiration making its first hesitant appearance on the tops of our fore-heads. At least the fall air was cooling quickly, and there was always a soft breeze in Oxford. I was glad we had given our-selves over an hour to get there, even though Vick had made it sound like it couldn't be more that a twenty-minute stroll.

We walked and walked, passing more little houses, the occasional pub, and eventually a series of expensive car deal-erships as the hill lessened and finally flattened out. And then suddenly we were in the country. It was as if someone had drawn a line across the road and announced, "From here on out there shall be no civilization!" A barn stood far off in the distance, in the midst of acres of mustard-colored rapeseed flowers. We stopped and stared.

It was dark long before we came across a little village of stone cottages, having turned around and chosen the other branch of the split, and then walked what seemed like miles and miles more. A woman with two small children was hur-rying by, the opposite direction we were traveling, and I stopped her. She wasn't sure, but she thought if we went over that bridge there would be a large field to our right and if we snuck through an opening in the hedge there should be a sort of footpath. If we followed that, we ought to be able to see the lights of the King's Arms from there.

She was right. A mist had begun to settle, and of course none of us had brought flashlights, but once we discerned the secret passage into the field, the distant glow of the pub beck-oned us like a lighthouse.

We arrived, hearts thumping, sweat dotting the underarms of our white shirts, feet aching (rule #1 of catering—always wear comfortable shoes, even if you don't think you'll be hiking for two hours prior to the job). Michael immediately ushered us upstairs to a large room with tables in tight rows, mostly already set with china and goblets. "We figured we better get going with the set-up," he said curtly, clearly annoyed at our tardiness, despite our effusive apologies and explanations. "Jill did a few of the napkins, but you can do the rest. And then . . ." He stopped himself, waving one hand dismissively, "Well, you know what you're doing." With that, he turned and left.

Monica and Lauren had never even waitressed before, and I had only served breakfast at a quaint Vermont B & B. Oh, and passed out spaghetti at an occasional church supper. But I didn't tell him that.

The napkins eluded us. We unfolded and refolded the ones Jill had left fanning crisply and elegantly from the mouths of the goblets, trying to determine the secret pattern. Every time we tried to assemble one from scratch it turned out like some sort of crossbreed of a broken accordion and a dead fish. They flopped limply, sagged over the rims, set the glasses off balance so that they tipped over and clanged against the silverware. And worse, my napkins looked as though a different disease plagued them than Lauren's, and hers were not the same sort of pathetic as Monique's. Finally, when the cook came out looking for us, we had to surrender, convinced that Jill must have been equipped with an iron and starch or some other advantage that we lacked.

There were two cooks, actually, who were operating out of a closet-sized hallway at the bottom of the back stairs. One of them was probably in his fifties, with a rounded stomach and graying whiskers. He wore a stained apron and barked orders in a Cockney accent to his younger sidekick, who was busily arranging arugula greens and drizzling vinaigrette onto salad plates. We could hear guests arriving upstairs, a muffled shuffling of feet and the dull buzz of distant conversation.

Quickly, we decided on a game plan, dividing the room up into thirds so that each of us would have our own section. I tried to take charge, to sound confident, since I was the one with "experience." Just give them their food and keep the wine glasses full, I told them. That's all there is to it.

Salad plates went down fine. It was tricky wedging ourselves between the tables—there were certain larger guests who barricaded the narrow passageways, making it simply impossible to reach anyone beyond them. But most everyone was obliging, passing down plates to the unreachables, scooting their chairs in as far as possible. The guests were overwhelmingly male, dressed in dark suits with an occasional gold cricket-themed pin glittering on a lapel. There were a few ladies scattered through the crowd, in long, full-skirted gowns. They were like centerpieces, one or two per table, a splash of color that was pleasing to the eye but never interfered with the boisterous camaraderie of the men folk.

I was clearing the small bread plates to make room for the main course when it happened. I slid between the two tightest tables, trying not to rub my backside against any of the fine gentlemen behind me as I leaned forward, reaching one arm between sets of shoulders to collect as many dishes as possible in one trip (I knew the cook would be thrusting plates stacked with beef Wellington at me as soon as I reached the bottom step of the stairs). Sometimes people see tragic things happen as if they were transpiring in slow motion. Well, I *felt* this in slow motion . . . the plate beginning to slip, its greasy edge sliding slowly from my index finger and thumb. I thought I could rescue it, get it over the woman's dark pile of hair and onto my stack safely, the close call gone undetected. Even in that brief, split second, I imagined myself telling Lauren and Monique later that night, after the whole event was behind us, that I had *almost* dropped a dish on this lady's head.

But fate would have it otherwise, sort of. The dish *did* graze over her head, but it left my grasp just beyond it, plummeting down between the back of her chair and the back of her white silk gown. I watched as the little leftover pat of butter stuck squarely against the small of her back. She stood up quickly with a little gasp, backing her chair into me where I stood, pinned in place and trying to balance the remaining dishes in one hand as embarrassment rose hotly in my cheeks. "Oh dear," I managed, because I had to say something to the indignant face that stared accusingly, too close to my own.

I tried to apologize, retrieve the plate, remove the butter with a cloth napkin, assess the damage, and extricate myself from my cage where I was becoming increasingly claustrophobic, all at once. I offered to bring her a damp cloth.

"Is it terribly bad?" she asked, her voice suddenly transformed to a whimper as she twisted around awkwardly, like a dog who wants to chase her tail but can't because it's being pulled along by a leash.

"No, no," I assured, willfully removing my gaze from the greasy yellowish splotch seeping into the delicate fabric, like a flower petal bruised by careless fingers.

I avoided her as much as possible for the rest of the evening, edging along the opposite side of the table, which meant being slapped on the rump by one or two increasingly inebriated, aging Brits, much to the amusement of the other chaps.

I never catered in Oxford again. Perhaps I would have if the Botley Catering Company hadn't gone out of business a few weeks later. But honestly, I wasn't ready to venture into that world again until two years later, when catering in New York became my biggest source of income, and where I served hors d'oeuvres at elitist restaurants, museums, and theaters for posh parties I would never have gotten into if I weren't dressed in a catering tuxedo. At that point, I began looking forward to my catering gigs . . . and I never forgot the danger of carrying more than three plates at once—*especially* butter plates.

The following jobs, from "Cater Waiter" to "Ice Cream Taster" to "Barista," are all food-related. So grab a snack (this might make you hungry) and enjoy.

39. Cater Waiter

<u>What You Do:</u> It's your job to set up for a party, serve the food, and cleanup/breakdown when it's over, along with a team of other waiters. You may be minimally involved in food preparation, but that's mostly up to the chefs.

<u>What You Get:</u> $12 to $20/hour, more for captains/managers. You might get some free food, too—I've come home with a whole glazed ham, full trays of fruit, strips of filet mignon, big chunks of gourmet cheese . . . and the list goes on.

<u>What It Costs:</u> Uniforms vary from casual (black dress pants, black shoes, white-collared shirt) to formal (tuxedo: $100 to $200).

<u>What You Need:</u> You don't have to be a genius to cater. However, you might have to shave off your beard, and if you have a bad back or you dislike people in a general sense, it's probably not the job for you.

<u>Perks</u>
• Hours are very flexible. Most companies will call you when they have a job and you decide if you want to do it or not.

• You might get to see some famous folks, especially if you're working parties in a metropolitan area like New York or Los Angeles. I've catered parties with guests including Richard Gere, Phillip Glass, Wynton Marsalis, Yoko Ono, and Sean Lennon (son of John).

Downsides

• If you see famous people, it's when you're filling their water glass or cleaning their puke off the floor. You're not at the party to socialize, and you're not likely to get any autographs.

• Work tends to be seasonable. Expect to get a lot of calls in June, November, and December. The rest of the year (especially January through April) you may have to look elsewhere for work.

Sites to Check Out

• **www.localcatering.com**—Type in your location to find a list of local catering companies.

• **www.101cateringtips.com** is geared toward the customer, but it includes listings of catering companies across the U.S.

LINGO

Sanit. Short for "sanitation," where all the dirty dishes and garbage go.

French Service. When the server carries a tray of food on one arm to a table and uses the free arm to offer each guest at a table its contents.

Plated Service. When the plates are filled in the kitchen before being pre-set on the table or served to the seated guests.

Sweep. Serving the guests as a team, working across the room table by table, rather than one or two people serving each table. This method ensures that a whole table receives their food at the same time.

40. Ice Cream Taster

<u>What You Do:</u> Ice cream tasters hold a few very important roles in the frozen dairy world. Taster Master Ray Karam's job is to experiment with new flavor combinations for the rapidly expanding chain Cold Stone. He dreams up a new idea, selects the appropriate mix-ins, and grabs a spoon, evaluating the concoction for flavor and its potential appeal to consumers. He is the proud originator of "Paradise Found," white chocolate ice cream with bananas, coconut, macadamia nuts, and pineapple. John Harrison, official taster for Edy's Grand Ice Cream, has more of a quality control position. Every morning he tests sixty packages of ice cream, making sure they are as fresh, tasty, and creamy as they can be. His taste buds are reportedly insured for a million dollars. Other tasters work for parlors that sell several brands of ice cream. Their job is to sample new varieties when they come in from the various companies that want their product represented in the store.

<u>What You Get:</u> The average salary for food scientists is $56,000.

<u>What It Costs:</u> Nothing

<u>What You Need:</u> I'm not going to lie and tell you any average Joe or Jill can march into an ice cream parlor and demand a job as an official taster. I mean, you could try it . . . confidence and a big smile go a long way sometimes. But most food scientists and taste testers have experience in the industry, and many of the best ones have chemistry degrees, oddly enough.

Perks
• I think this is pretty obvious. We're talking about getting paid to eat ice cream on a daily basis.

Downsides
• What pleases the taste buds does not always please the waistline. Harrison gets around this by spitting out the ice cream before actually swallowing. Seems like kind of a waste, but hey, you gotta do what you gotta do.

• Serious ice cream tasters don't allow themselves to eat anything spicy within twenty-four hours of a taste test.

Sites to Check Out
• **www.chow.com/stories/10008** is a good outline of what to consider when judging ice cream.

• **www.2dips.com**—If you think you can break into the tasting business, make sure you know your facts first. This site will get you started.

HOW DO YOU GET THE JOB?

Many ice cream companies list job openings on their Web sites. If you don't find "Ice Cream Tester" specifically, look for anything that seems related (e.g. "quality assurance specialist" or "product scientist") and send a query to the contact provided. If there's a phone number listed, call and ask who to direct an application to. You might get laughed at, or you might end up with a sweet job (pun intended).

41. Scenic Caterer

<u>What You Do:</u> Prepare a gourmet meal or picnic for two and serve it in a beautiful, romantic location, such as on the beach, in a garden or park, or near a lake with a view of the mountains. Scenic catering is popular for special occasions such as engagements (what's more romantic then proposing after dinner under a palm tree as the sun sets over the ocean?), anniversaries, or for any guy who really wants to impress a girl. Menus can be adjusted to match the circumstances—if you're serving a picnic, the meal can be less formal than if you're setting up a table with a white linen cloth, fine china, and real silver. Regardless of how elegant the meal, you'll want to include candles, flowers, goblets for wine, bug spray, and (if there's any chance of it getting chilly when the sun goes down), a light blanket or shawl.

<u>What You Get:</u> $200 to $500/meal, depending on what you serve and the formality of the occasion.

<u>What It Costs:</u> Besides food, you'll need a table, two chairs, candles, dishes, goblets, silver, basic cooking equipment, Bunsen burners to keep food hot, a car or van to carry the supplies to the destination, and other miscellaneous supplies to keep your guests comfortable (see above). Chances are, you already have many of these things or can buy them used, which will mean that, except for the van, you should be able to get going for $100 to $200.

What You Need
• Ability to cook

• Knowledge of serving (you'll want to be proper if it's a formal dinner).

Perks
• Since you'll only be serving two people, you won't need industrial cooking equipment or wholesale shipments of ingredients.

• While the couple is eating, you can chill out and read a book or enjoy the scenery (preferably in a place where you can see them but they can't see you). You'll want to check on them every so often and refill their wine, but it's not like at a restaurant where you have to be constantly on the go.

Downsides
• Couples in love tend to want romantic evenings to go on forever, which might mean you're waiting for them for hours on end, unless you can find a way to politely suggest they take a walk or go somewhere else. It's never a good idea to offer to transport the guests to and from the location along with the food and supplies, because then you really are stuck there until they want to leave.

Sites to Check Out
• **www.redballoondays.com.au/category/Gourmet /dinner-date**—This site has a variety of creative catering advertisements. Browse the various descriptions to gain inspiration, ideas of how much to charge, etc.

- **www.lovingyou.com/content/cooking/** gives romantic recipes for two, like "broiled halibut with strawberry mint salsa" and "white chocolate fig kisses."

- **www.foodsafety.gov**—Official advice for safe cooking.

42. Dishwasher

<u>What You Do:</u> It's your job to wash, dry, and put away all the dishes produced by the restaurant/café/bakery. This includes the plates, silverware, glasses, etc. used by the guests, as well as the bowls, cutting boards, pans, etc. used by the cooks. Most of the dishes can go through an electric dishwasher, which takes less than a minute per load. Larger dishes will need to be washed by hand.

<u>What You Get:</u> Minimum wage to $10/hour, plus maybe a free meal.

<u>What It Costs:</u> Nothing

<u>What You Need:</u> Ability to work quickly and efficiently. Some pots are heavy, so muscles are a plus.

<u>Perks</u>
- Make friends with the cooks and you can probably score some free food. My boyfriend and I worked at a local Italian restaurant when we lived in Kauai. He was the dishwasher and I worked the cash register. Whenever I went back in the kitchen,

he had a plate of stuffed mushrooms or hot arti-
choke dip and bread. At the end of the night we left
stocked with pasta, salads, or pizza. Since we were
camping on the beach and were guaranteed a solid
meal every night we worked, even though the pay
wasn't great we were easily able to break even.

• Wherever there are restaurants, there is a need for
  dishwashers. Dishwashing jobs are not hard to
  come by.

Downsides
• Although the job doesn't require any particular
  skills or intellectual capacity, it is often fast-paced
  and can be stressful when the dish pile is suddenly
  so tall it's casting a shadow over the whole
  kitchen. You will be tired after your shift.

• Plan to have hands that strongly resemble prunes.

• Conditions in a kitchen can be hot—be careful of
  steam or hot water burns. And while you're at it,
  try not to slip on the wet floor.

Sites to Check Out
• **www.indeed.com** has an extensive list of dish-
  washing job openings.

• **www.metrokc.gov/health/foodsfty/mockinspec-
  tion9.htm**—Learn what health inspectors look for
  when visiting commercial kitchens.

TIPS

• The best way to find a dishwashing job is to go to
  restaurants and offer your services.

• Wear old clothes or a full apron—oftentimes bleach is
  used in kitchens for sterilization, which can wreak
  havoc on your clothes.

43. Barista

<u>What You Do:</u> Take orders, make gourmet coffee (lattes, cappuccino, etc.), serve, count out change, repeat. Opening and closing shifts will require additional tasks—turning on or shutting off coffeemakers, wiping down counters, mopping the floor, etc.

<u>What You Get:</u> $7 to $12/hour. Some coffeehouses (like Starbucks) offer health insurance if you work 20 hours or more.

<u>What It Costs:</u> Nothing

<u>What You Need:</u> Minimal. Some coffeehouses might want you to have experience, but most will allow newbies if you're friendly, responsible, and they need the help.

<u>Perks</u>
- Hand over a good cup of Joe and you've just made somebody's morning.

- Coffeehouses tend to have a pleasant, hip atmosphere, even if you're behind the counter madly steaming milk and grinding beans.

Downsides
- If you're on the morning shift, you'll probably have to start at stupid o'clock in the morning.

- Chain coffeehouses (e.g. Starbucks) double as community centers. Everyone knows they can run into a Starbucks to use the bathroom, get out of the rain or snow, or pull out their laptop and get to work. This is all well and good until people start taking advantage of the system (which will happen approximately two minutes after you unlock the door and hang the "open" sign). Starbucks, for example, has had to make a "no sleeping" rule to discourage tired patrons from bunking in the corners. My friend (and Starbucks manager veteran) Emily also tells about a woman who, rather than standing in line to use the restroom, regularly wet herself in the chairs, moving from seat to seat when the puddles became uncomfortable. Another fellow decided it best to just let loose in the corner. And more than one junky has overdosed in the stall, requiring a call to the fire department to come pick the lock and drag the victim to the hospital.

Sites to Check Out
- **www.coffeegeek.com**—Learn to make special brews, analyze consumer reviews, and read about coffee in the news.

- **www.starbucks.com**—Click on "career center" for employment information.

44. Fast Food Worker

<u>What You Do:</u> Greet customers, take their orders, give them their food in exchange for their money—it's relatively straightforward. You may do some food preparation, and if you're on the opening or closing shifts there will be setup or cleanup to do.

<u>What You Get:</u> $6 to $12/hour.

<u>What It Costs:</u> Nothing

<u>What You Need:</u> Usually all you need is proof that you can legally hold a job (and sometimes that's negotiable).

<u>Perks</u>
• You'll meet some interesting people (that's an understatement).

<u>Downsides</u>
• There is a negative stigma attached to fast food restaurants and the people who work at them. Basically, it's true. Unless you land a job at one of the few fast food joints that specializes in fresh ingredients (like Subway), you will work with low quality food, frying pre-cut potatoes in oil that's been used over and over, greeting drive-through customers with the same rote script

("Welcome to Burger Land. Can I take your order?"), and mindlessly punching orders into a computer screen. At the end of the day you'll mop up the floor, wipe the grease off the counters, go home, shower, and crash.

Sites to Check Out
- **www.fastfood.com**—Learn all about fast food franchises and fill out an application that potential employers can look at (though I imagine you'd have better luck going directly to a restaurant and filling out an application in person).

- **www.foodwork.com**—Pretty much the same deal, only at this site you can search for all kinds of restaurant jobs—not just fast food chains.

45. Gustatory Athlete

<u>What You Do:</u> Also known as a gurgitator or an epi-cureator, you will enter contests in which the goal is to eat as much as you can as fast as you can. There are all sorts of foods you can scarf for cash: pizza, chicken wings, hamburgers, grapes, cheesecakes, cow brains, pancakes, reindeer sausages, tiramisu . . . you name it, there's a contest for it. Eating contests usually take place at fairs or festivals and many are seasonally themed, such as corned beef and cab-bage eating competitions around St. Patrick's Day.

<u>What You Get:</u> On a local level, you might only get a free meal or a T-shirt for your efforts, but the big time eaters win up to $30,000 a contest.

What It Costs: Entry fees are generally around $20.

What You Need: You really have to be able to pack it away in order to make any money at this. You'll be up against some tough competition. Thirty-nine-year-old, 105-pound Sonya Thomas has set more than fifteen records, including 8.4 pounds of baked beans in 2 minutes and 47 seconds. Don Lerman managed to get down 7 sticks of salted butter in exactly five minutes.

Perks
• Even if you don't win, $20 for all-you-can-eat isn't that bad. You'd pay more at a Manhattan deli.

Downsides
• If you throw up and any of it lands on the table or your plate, you get the boot.

Sites to Check Out
• **www.ifoce.com**—The International Federation of Competitive Eating should be your first point of reference.

• **http://people.howstuffworks.com/competitive-eating.htm**—Learn more about some of the top competitors and how they've made it where they are today.

• **www.competitiveeaters.com**—You'll find more competition listings and photos here at the home of "picnic style rules," regulations that deter competitive eaters from dunking, mashing, or otherwise mutilating food to make it more easily consumable.

46. Hot Dog Vendor

<u>What You Do:</u> Set up a stand, cart, or van in a public area and cook and sell hot dogs. You'll want to offer drinks, too, and possibly chips, ice cream, or other snacks. At the hot dog stand my family ran in Vermont, we experimented with introducing things like hot cider and apple pie slices in the fall, or other treats like Oreos and candy, but we always came back to the fact that most people go to a hot dog stand for hot dogs.

<u>What You Get:</u> The busiest hot dog vendors in Manhattan make up to $100,000/year. A reasonably successful business in a less trafficked area can hope to make a profit of $100 to $300/day, or somewhere in the vicinity of $30,000 to $80,000/year.

<u>What It Costs:</u> Costs will depend on what sort of facilities you want. You can get a basic cart for around $2,500 (or less if you buy it used), or a fancy super-duper trailer for $20,000 or more. Plan on another $1,000 for licensing and initial inventory.

<u>What You Need:</u> You'll need some basic business sense and perseverance to make a hot dog business (or any business) work. Chances are you won't make it big in your first few months, but give it some time and you might be surprised how much cash the little wieners start raking in.

Perks
- All the hot dogs you can eat! (Of course, every hot dog you consume cuts down on your revenue, but when you're buying them wholesale, a couple of dogs a day won't drain your account.)

Downsides
- Weather will have a significant effect on your business. There aren't too many people who like to stand in line outside for lunch when it's rainy and cold.

Sites to Check Out
- **www.uscarts.net/startingahotdogstand.html**—Here you can glean some useful tidbits on starting a hot dog business, shop for a cart, and read related articles.

- **www.allamericanhotdog.com**—This site is a little overwhelming at first glance—there's a lot of information in a rather jumbled format—but it's a good place to shop for equipment and supplies.

Chapter Four

COUNTRY PURSUITS

Christmas Tree Farmer

Fire Lookout
Beekeeper
Human Scarecrow
Haying
Raising Hens
Christmas Tree Farmer
Fish Sampler
Worm Farmer

*Farming looks mighty easy when your plow is a pencil,
and you're a thousand miles from the corn field.*

—Dwight D. Eisenhower

47. Fire Lookout

<u>What You Do:</u> Sit high up in a tower on a hilltop and watch the surrounding area for forest fires. If you spot anything suspiciously red or smoky amongst the evergreens, you radio the local Emergency Communications Center (ECC), where help can be quickly dispatched.

<u>What You Get:</u> $7 to $10/hour

<u>What It Costs:</u> Nothing, although you'll probably be living in a primitive cabin in the middle of the deep woods, so you better get yourself a sleeping bag, a flashlight, and some good camp food.

<u>What You Need:</u> Many lookouts come from a background of firefighting, but this isn't a requirement. You should, however, be the sort of person who likes a lot of alone time.

<u>Perks</u>
• As Donna Ashworth of the Woody Mountain Lookout on the Coconino National Forest says, "It's hard to make a fool of yourself when you're by yourself."

• Amazing views, all day long.

<u>Downsides</u>
• Forest fires often begin during lightning storms, which means you must be up in your tall metal tower on top of the tall mountain, in the worst of the electrical fury. Fire towers are built with wooden floors and equipped with lightning rods,

but unfortunately that's really no guarantee against the wrath of the thunder gods.

- There's a fine line between peaceful solitude and miserable isolation—if you're not a loner by nature, you may find yourself quickly crossing that line.

Sites to Check Out
- **www.firelookout.org**—Job listings, stories, links, history, Smoky the Bear patches . . . what more could you possibly be looking for?

- **www.geocities.com/rainforest/jungle/5057/ questions.html** is a very helpful article by a fire lookout.

- **www.wildfirenews.com** offers more job listings and all sorts of international wildfire-related links and articles.

48. Beekeeper

<u>What You Do:</u> If you happen to be of British ancestry, the beekeeping lifestyle might come quite naturally to you—basically you smoke, keep an eye on the queen, manipulate the colonies, and collect the goods (no offense . . . I'm an Anglophile if there ever was one). Actually, there's a fair amount you should know about bees if you're going to be successful, including how to prevent swarming, how to be sure there's adequate food to keep the buzzers around, and, of course, how to not get stung to death (you'll definitely get stung at least a few times, but you don't want the whole colony to rebel). You should certainly do your research—at

the very least visit the sites listed below—and you might consider apprenticing under a commercial beekeeper for a while to learn the tricks of the trade.

<u>What You Get:</u> The low end of adult salaries for a beekeeper in a commercial setting is $20,000. If you're starting your own business, keep in mind that an average hive produces 20 to 30 pounds of surplus honey in a season, which you could sell for roughly $75. This isn't much, but if you get several hives going, you can produce a lot more, and your income is virtually all profit once you have the equipment. In addition, there are all sorts of other bee products you can sell: one in three bites of food you put in your mouth contains ingredients produced directly or indirectly by bees (or so I'm told). Wax is the second most commonly sold bee product, but pollen is also gaining popularity as a health product.

<u>What It Costs:</u> $250 to $500, depending on what you make versus what you buy (find instructions for making your own hive at a link below). You'll need at least two hives with bees, a bee suit and veil, a smoker, gloves, and a honey extractor.

<u>What You Need:</u> You'll need a rural area with plenty of flowers nearby to keep your bees happy.

<u>Perks</u>
• There's little in this world sweeter than fresh, unfiltered honey, and it has some amazing health properties, too.

- During winter months, beekeeping requires little to no work.

- Bee stings can help prevent arthritis (which is great for the "eat the crust first" sort of people who prefer to deal with pain now if it means they won't have to do so later).

Downsides
- If you're one of those people who would rather put off pain altogether in the hopes that there will be a cure for arthritis by the time you get it, there's really nothing good about a bee sting.

Sites to Check Out
- **www.beemaster.com**—Everything beekeeping-related

- **www.sfc.ucdavis.edu/pubs/SFNews/archive/94032.htm** is an excellent article on starting a small beekeeping operation.

- **www.farmcentre.com/download/downloads/beekeeper_business_plan_e.pdf**—This is a thorough guide to the business end of beekeeping.

- **www.beesource.com/plans/index.htm** has plans for building all sorts of beehives.

49. Human Scarecrow

What You Do: Frighten birds away from valuable crops. Crows tend to be the worst villains, but magpies and other fowl are also known for damaging fruit and vegetable crops, and even robbing poultry of their eggs.

What You Get: $10 to $15/hour

What It Costs: Nothing

What You Need: Ability to wave your arms, holler, spray the hose, or come up with other ways of dissuading the winged beasts from landing on the crops.

Perks
• You'll have plenty of time to work on your tan.

Downsides
• Getting pecked by angry crows

Sites to Check Out
• **www.agnet.org/library/article/nc126b.html**—This article will teach you the basics and explain the importance of the scarecrow profession.

• **http://icwdm.org/handbook/birds/Magpies. asp**—Learn about the damage magpies can do and how to stop them.

• **www.banthecannons.com/high-tech.html**—Familiarize yourself with the competition (bird-scaring robots).

50. Haying

<u>What You Do:</u> If you already have tall grass growing in your field/yard, all you'll have to do is cut it down and bale it (unless you can find a buyer who wants it loose or in bags, which is possible if you're selling small quantities to local farmers). If your meadow is more like a junk yard, you will need to clear the area of debris and seed it with alfalfa, clover, oats, or similar grasses, depending on your location and the pH of your soil—check with other local farmers to see what they're growing. For a yard that is less than an acre, you can cut it with a scythe and gather it with a forage rake and a pitchfork. A sickle-bar mower works well for cutting a slightly larger plot, and if you're haying a whole field you'll want a ride-on tractor.

<u>What You Get:</u> $2 to $6/bale, depending on where you live and what type of grass you are cutting.

<u>What It Costs:</u> This will depend on how large your lot is, and consequently, what equipment you need. If you don't already own a tractor, I wouldn't recommend buying one if your aim is to make a profit off of a few acres—by the time you sell enough hay to cover the cost of the tractor (which compare in price to lower-end cars), you'll probably need a new one. Instead, use a mower or a scythe, as mentioned above. You should be able to find a used sickle-bar mower for $200 to $300; a decent used baler for somewhere in the neighborhood of $1,000; and a hay rake for $500. For a large crop you will need a pickup truck or wagon to transport the bales.

<u>What You Need:</u> If you have the land and the energy to get out there and do the work, you can hay.

<u>Perks</u>
• Get paid for keeping your land from growing into a jungle.

<u>Downsides</u>
• The cost of gas will eat into your profits.

• Wet weather can ruin hay crops. You can't bail wet hay—it will mold, making it inedible for many animals and a potential fire hazard.

<u>Sites to Check Out</u>
• **www.sheepscreek.com/rural/haying.html**— This site answers the most common questions about the haying process.

• **www.ca.uky.edu/agc/pubs/agr/agr26/agr26. htm**—If you need to fertilize or otherwise rejuvenate your field, check out this link.

• **www.woolfarm.com/makinghay.htm**—Haying from a farmer's perspective

51. Raising Hens

<u>What You Do:</u> Chickens are good for a lot of things (meat, weed control, nitrogen-rich manure), but the simplest and least disgusting way to make money from feathered fowl is probably gathering and selling hens' eggs. You'll need to keep your hens in an area

protected from rain, wind, and extreme temperatures. They like to have a ledge they can comfortably perch on to sleep and separate nesting boxes for laying eggs. During the summer, chickens can run around the yard and forage for most of their food, but during winter months you may need to supply more feed, depending on how cold it gets where you live. In Kauai, chickens roam the island year round, perfectly happy to take care of themselves (with a little help from generous tourists with extra snacks). You'll want to collect the eggs every day, and you can sell them to family, neighbors, or at a farm stand.

<u>What You Get:</u> I'll be honest. You won't make a fortune raising a few hens in your backyard. But this book is about making an extra buck, and that I can pretty safely promise you. Free-range fresh eggs can go for $2 to $4/dozen, and hens generally lay between 200 and 250 eggs per year. You can expect to make a profit of somewhere in the vicinity of $50/year per hen.

<u>What It Costs:</u> This will depend on how big a roost you want and how much the hens will fend for themselves for food. For six hens, you can plan on spending about $20 to $25 per year on each hen (this covers the cost of the hens, the feed, basic equipment like a water dispenser, and the housing—building your own shed will save money, as will allowing the hens access to a natural water source and an area to forage). If you buy more hens, the cost of living per hen will go down, and the number of eggs you can sell will increase.

<u>What You Need:</u> You'll need a place to keep your hens and some time to care for them. If you only have a few hens, it shouldn't take more than ten minutes a day to keep them healthy and happy.

Perks
• A steady supply of fresh eggs (and believe me, fresh eggs are like a different food group than the flavorless little white things that come in a carton at the store).

Downsides
• Foxes, wild dogs, and even hawks love to eat chicken as much as any of us do.

Sites to Check Out
• **www.accidentalsmallholder.net/articles/poultry**—An excellent introduction to raising hens.

• **www.gatewaytovermont.com/thefarm/coop.htm**—And another one, in case you still have questions.

• **http://poultryone.com** includes related links and other useful information.

52. Christmas Tree Farmer

What You Do: In March, you dig up the thawing ground and plant seedlings. Then you wait 7 to 15 years. Well, maybe only 3 to 6 years if you live in southern states, but still, this is not an instant gratification sort of job. Every June you'll have to go around and prune the trees to keep them in tip-top Christmas tree form. And every so often you'll want to mow the grass between the trees, and maybe spray pesticides. When December rolls around, you can either harvest the trees, load them on a truck, and take them somewhere to sell, or you can have customers come right to the farm, pick out the tree they want, and then chop it down for them—or even give them a saw and let them do the work.

<u>What You Get:</u> Christmas trees sell at about $30 for a medium-sized one in rural areas. Anywhere near a city they sell for three times as much.

<u>What It Costs:</u> An initial investment of $300 to $400, for about 30 trees: 30 balsam fir seedlings for $50, a backpack pesticide sprayer and pesticides for $100 to $200, a shearing knife and clippers for about $100, fertilizer for around $10 to $15. After you purchase the equipment, your annual costs will go way down. If you need a truck or a lawnmower, you'll obviously have to shell out a lot more.

<u>What You Need:</u> You'll need at least a few acres of land, patience, and the ability to keep up regular physical labor.

<u>Perks</u>
- You can put into this job as much or as little as you want to. Plant a dozen trees and keep another full time job, or plant thirty acres and put your heart and soul into it.

- The satisfaction of seeing tiny seedlings grow into beautiful trees that will thrill little kids and parents at Christmastime.

<u>Downsides</u>
- You only receive an income for a month out of the year, which will make the first couple of years especially difficult if you're depending on this for your main income. Some farms have taken to giving tours during the rest of the year to increase their earnings.

Sites to Check Out

- **www.urbanforest.org**—This site has tons of information on growing trees. Click on "50 Careers in Trees" for a section on Christmas tree farming.

- **www.musserforests.com**—You can buy all sorts of seedlings here.

- **www.greenbeam.com/branchsmith** has links to a variety of horticulture supplies and equipment.

53. Fish Sampler

What You Do: The old-fashioned method (which is still frequently employed) is to sit in a viewing station attached to a dam and watch fish swim up the ladder. When you see a fish, you press a button, which will add it to the official count. You might get to measure a fish occasionally, which involves capturing the fish in a tank that has had the oxygen sucked out of it and holding it captive until it stops squirming. Once it's still, you can put a tape measure to it before returning it to a recuperation tank. Finally the fish gets tagged and released back onto the ladder to continue its journey. More and more samplers are using electrofishing, which involves pulling an insulated electric wire attached to a portable generator through a river. The fish are stunned and almost magically drawn to the wire, at which point you catch them in a net and take them to a holding place for measuring and weighing before returning them to the stream.

What You Get: $8 to $15/hour

<u>What It Costs:</u> Nothing

<u>What You Need:</u> Although a background in marine science might land you a job more quickly, there are no specific prerequisites for becoming a fish sampler.

<u>Perks</u>
- You will learn a lot about marine life, and possibly other sorts of wildlife. Tim Lawrence, a former fish counter in Vermont, remembers seeing, among other things, multiple bald eagles while working.

<u>Downsides</u>
- When there aren't bald eagles swirling above your head, staring at the water and occasionally tapping a red button can get old fast.

- An increasing number of checkpoints are using sonar to count fish, which means jobs in this area are increasingly difficult to come by.

<u>Sites to Check Out</u>
- **www.sf.adfg.state.ak.us**—Salmon counting is especially popular in Alaska. Explore this site for related links and articles.

- **www.wyomingfishing.net/ft_count.htm**—Learn more about electrofishing here.

- **www.admin.mtu.edu/urel/news/media_ relations/181/**—Hydroacoustics . . . yet another way to count our floppy friends.

54. Worm Farmer

<u>What You Do:</u> To start, build a wooden box, two feet by three feet by one foot deep. Drill a quarter-inch hole every three inches along the bottom and sides to allow for moisture to escape and air to flow easily. Cover the bottom with aged manure. You can also add coconut fiber or peat moss, but you should soak it for a while first and then squeeze it out before adding it to the bedding. Find or buy some worms and drop them in (red worms are best, but they might be hard to find in your backyard). Next, add some worm food—ideally, fruit and vegetable scraps cut into quarter-inch strips and partially composted. You can also add tea bags, shredded paper, or straw, but absolutely no meat or dairy or salt. Crushed up eggshells are good, too. Then tuck the creepy crawlers in with a piece of burlap laid over the top. When the box is full of more worms and bedding and decomposed food, dig down about six inches with a pitchfork and pull out the worms. Transplant some into a new box, or clean out the castings (waste products), sell it as fertilizer, and start with a new bed in the same box (worms don't like to live in their own waste for too long—can you blame them?). Pack the rest in damp peat moss in a breathable bag (paper bags work), bring them to the nearest tackle shop, and you're in business!

<u>What You Get:</u> One pound of worms goes for about $20 (but keep in mind that it takes a lot of worms to get a pound). Worm populations quadruple in about six months. Five pounds of castings go for $10 to $15.

<u>What It Costs:</u> $15 to $25 for worms and the wood to buy the box (if you have old scraps of wood around, all the better!).

<u>What You Need:</u> Lack of squeamishness.

<u>Perks</u>
• Worms are the easiest pets/employees you'll ever have. You don't have to walk them, litter box train them, brush them, milk them, or buy them food (they're perfectly happy to eat your scraps). They'll work all day for you, eating and making babies, and they won't complain a bit!

• Your kitchen waste will be cut down significantly.

<u>Downsides</u>
• Worm farms can start to stink if you overfeed them.

<u>Sites to Check Out</u>
• **www.deckerwormsales.com**—You can buy worms here to get you started. There are also some good tips for keeping your worms happy and healthy.

• **www.acmewormfarm.com**—This site tells about worm composting as well as commercial vermi-culture. You can buy everything you'll need here (including an Acme Worm Farm apron—surely a necessity).

• **www.newfarm.org/features/0903/worms/ index.shtml**—This is an interesting article about a successful commercial worm farmer.

Chapter Five

TRAVEL AND ADVENTURE

Commercial Skydiving

Commercial Fishing Crew in Alaska
Kibbutz in Israel
Ski Lift Operator
Trail Building/Maintenance
Shell Picking in Kauai
Group Adventure Leader
Resort Receptionist
Work on a Cruise Ship
Kayak Tour Guide off San Juan Island
Commercial Skydiving in New Zealand
FEMA Disaster Assistance Employee
Dog Handler in Alaska
Harvester in Australia
English Teacher Abroad
Snowmaker

Adventure can be an end in itself. Self-discovery
is the secret ingredient that fuels daring.

—Katie Martin

55. Commercial Fishing Crew in Alaska

<u>What You Do:</u> Catch salmon, crabs, halibut, or other fish, depending on the season, off the coast of Alaska. As a deckhand, you will be working irregular hours baiting hooks, lugging 40- to 60-pound anchors, coiling heavy fishing line, possibly hacking ice off the boat and washing down the decks.

<u>What You Get:</u> Deckhands usually make 1.5 percent to 10 percent of the adjusted gross catch (in other words, the more fish you haul out of the ocean, the more money you put in your pocket). Some boats offer a daily rate of $50 to $100 instead. Look online and you will find stories about novice crew hands earning $80,000 in eight months, but it's not likely you'll make more than $2,000 a month, if that.

<u>What It Costs:</u>
- $200 to $300 for gear: quality rain jacket and pants, rubber boots, gloves, wrist covers, and a sleeping bag.

- $175 for a commercial fishing crew license ($60 if you are an Alaska resident).

- Plus, of course, however much it will cost to get yourself to Alaska.

<u>What You Need:</u> You must be able bodied and a hard worker—this is a very physically demanding job. You should also be able to get along amicably with a crew, even when you're wet, cold, tired, and all stuck on a small boat for days at a time.

Perks
- Accommodations are often provided as part of the deal.

- Alaska is incredibly beautiful.

Downsides
- Commercial fishing in Alaska is recognized as one of the most hazardous jobs in the nation. In 1991 a Commercial Fishing Vessel Safety Act took effect, requiring boats to carry certain safety and survival instruments, but buoys and a life jacket are really no match for storms at sea. Still, when considering a job, be sure that safety precautions are being followed. Use common sense: if a boat looks cruddy and unkempt, think about whether its owner is the one you want to trust with your life. A sloppy boat may mean sloppy safety standards.

- The demand for canned salmon has gone down significantly over the last decade, making salmon fishing jobs more difficult to come by.

- Many people find the harsh fishing methods and general lack of respect for sea life disheartening, if not disgusting. If you're a naturalist or have ever even considered becoming a vegetarian, this is probably not the job for you.

Sites to Check Out
- **www.labor.state.ak.us/esd_alaska_jobs/ seafood.htm**—The Alaska Department of Labor offers useful information and job listings.

- **www.admin.adfg.state.ak.us/license/** has information on obtaining a license.

• **www.jobmonkey.com/kagwa** offers more job listings.

• **www.alaska-summer-jobs.com** includes details specific to various types of fishing.

HOW DO YOU GET THE JOB?

To get a position, most people wander up and down the docks talking to skippers and hoping someone else quits so they can take their place. Towns frequented by such hopefuls include Kodiak, Ketchikan, Homer, and Petersburg. Without experience to make you a more promising candidate for hire (and because living expenses in Alaska are high and you don't want to be stuck up there bumming around without a job for too long), you might be better off trying to secure a position before you go, using the resources listed here (or similar ones).

56. Kibbutz in Israel

<u>What You Do:</u> A kibbutz community is a place where volunteers, often from all over the world, work in exchange for room, board, and a small stipend. Types of work vary from picking dates to fishing to greeting guests at a tourist health spa to washing and folding laundry. You will have a chance to make your work preferences known, but there's a good chance that your top choice is also the first pick of a dozen other hopefuls. Volunteers have to agree to work where they are needed, even if it means shoveling cow dung. Most volunteers

stay for two to six months and work eight hours a day, six days a week. For your time off, many kibbutzim now have pubs, tennis courts, swimming pools, and offer occasional sightseeing excursions.

<u>What You Get:</u> A place to stay (probably in a dorm-like setting), three meals a day, medical care if needed, and around $80 a month.

<u>What It Costs:</u> Some kibbutzim require a deposit of $50 to $100 when you first arrive but return it to you after a couple of months (at which point, hopefully, you've convinced them you're not going to steal or permanently damage any of their property).

<u>What You Need:</u> You should be able and willing to work hard at whatever tasks you are given and be the sort of person who will enjoy living, working, and playing with the same people day in and day out.

Perks
- This is a wonderful way to get a taste of life in Israel without having to worry about where you'll stay or how you'll get around. Basically all of your needs will be provided for (often including stationery, tea, and sometimes even cigarettes and condoms), and you'll have a built-in community of friends.

- The social life in kibbutzim tends to be very active. Some kibbutzim even have onsite discos.

Downsides

• Israel's currently listed on the Department of State Web site as one of the most dangerous places for Americans to visit, and, considering that it's been a hotbed of conflict for thousands of years, chances are it will be on that list for awhile.

• Living in close quarters with multiple roommates always presents some challenges, and, depending on where you end up, the housing conditions can be pretty "basic" (i.e., a concrete hut with thin plastic walls serving as dividers between rooms).

• Saturday, the Sabbath, will be your day off, but it's also everyone else's day off, which makes it difficult to travel.

Sites to Check Out

• **www.kibbutz.org.il/eng/**—This site has all the details on what to expect, contact information, and an open forum for volunteers from all over the world that will give you some valuable insight into the kibbutzim lifestyle (especially if you're multilingual).

• **www.kibbutz.com**—This site is similar to the one above, but it never hurts to compare resources.

57. Ski Lift Operator

What You Do: If you've ever been down a ski slope, first you took the lift up. Before you sat down on the swinging chair that would whisk you away to the peak, someone probably grabbed it, slowed it down, and steadied it for you while you perched. And if you've had the unfortunate experience of losing your balance and landing on your rump, or dropping a pole just as the chair was coming up behind you, hopefully someone pushed a button and suddenly the buzz quieted and the chairs slowed to a halt. Well, that someone could be you.

<u>What You Get:</u> $7 to $9/hour, and hopefully a season pass.

<u>What It Costs:</u> Nothing

<u>What You Need:</u> You have to be moderately strong, as the chairs are heavy and oftentimes come pretty fast. Customer service experience is helpful—you might be expected to greet guests and check their passes, or keep the masses from breaking into chaos as they wait their turn.

<u>Perks</u>
• You get to be a ski bum on your time off.

• Discounts at the ski/snowboard shop

<u>Downsides</u>
• Cold

• Cold

• Sometimes very cold

<u>Sites to Check Out</u>
• **www.coolworks.com/ski-resort-jobs**—Find links to employment opportunities at ski resorts across the U.S.

- **www.natives.co.uk** lists ski-related jobs all over the world.

- **www.skiingthenet.com** includes more jobs listings.

58. Trail Building/Maintenance

<u>What You Do:</u> Work with a team to clear brush, construct bridges, mark trails, build steps, chop up and haul away fallen trees—anything having to do with hiking trail maintenance. You might camp with your team along the trail, stay at a base, or travel to work from your own accommodations.

<u>What You Get:</u> $10 to $15/hour for unskilled labor. If you know what you're doing (e.g., you can design bridges that won't collapse into the rushing river) and you've had experience, you can make more as a crew leader.

<u>What It Costs:</u> Nothing

<u>What You Need:</u> This is rigorous outdoor work, so you should be physically prepared to climb, haul, dig, and sweat.

<u>Perks</u>
- Spending time outdoors in nature

- Lots of exercise

- Opportunity to make some great friends

Downsides
- As with any outdoor job, bad weather can make a bad day.

- Because there are many volunteers for this sort of work, it can be hard to find paid positions—but they're out there, so keep looking.

Sites to Check Out
- **www.trailbuilders.org**—The Professional Trail Builder's Association has useful descriptions of what trail contractors do, as well as job listings.

- **www.americantrails.org**—Find related articles, training resources, and an excellent glossary of trail terms.

- **www.coolworks.com/conservation-corps-jobs/**—This site lists job openings for state and national conservation corps. Check out the other job categories while you're there—there are some great outdoor job ideas, as well as internship and opportunities for youth.

59. Shell Picking in Kauai

What You Do: Kahelelani, or Ni'ihau shells, are tiny pink treasures of the sea that are found only on the Hawaiian islands of Kauai and Ni'ihau. Since Ni'ihau is accessible only to native Hawaiians, the beaches of Kauai are the only places where most of us can get them. Shell picking requires a lot of time on your knees in the sand as you sort the Kahelelanis from the "imposters" (shells that look deceptively similar but will crush between your fingernails, making them inappropriate for use in jewelry).

<u>What You Get:</u> Around $100 for a film canister full of shells (about a day's work worth), if sold to a jeweler. One girl I know left for Kauai with $50 in her pocket. She camped on the beach while she picked shells and ended up trading four canisters of shells for a van, which she lived in for several months before settling in an apartment.

<u>What It Costs:</u> You can find flights from the West Coast to Kauai for under $500. Once you get there, I recommend setting up a tent at one of the island's designated beachside parks. It will only cost you $3 a night, and your view will be nicer than from any ritzy hotel room.

<u>What You Need:</u> Patience—these shells are not much bigger than a few grains of sand, so the progress is slow and sometimes tedious.

<u>Perks</u>
- The beaches of Kauai are some of the most beautiful in the world.

- You'll get a fabulous tan in a short amount of time (if it's not raining . . .).

<u>Downsides</u>
- Kauai is home to Mt. Waialeale, one of the wettest spots on earth, which means there's a pretty good chance you'll get rained on. When I lived there for a short while, it rained for forty-two days straight, and I was camping. But the waterfalls were amazing!

Sites to Check Out
- **www.niihaushellart.com/creation.html**—This gallery offers some useful background information on the shells.

- **www.kauai-hawaii.com** will help to familiarize you with the island before you decide to go.

60. Group Adventure Leader

What You Do: Can you see yourself surfing with a bunch of fifteen-year-olds off the coasts of Tahiti? How about backpacking across Central America, or constructing homes with twenty students in rural Thailand? More and more programs are popping up all over the world that encourage travel, adventure, community service, conflict resolution, and multicultural understanding. Every group needs a leader—someone who can tell the others what's going on, look out for the safety of the group, smooth over interpersonal tensions, coordinate activities, and be so much fun that everyone wants to hang out with you and do what you say. It's a tall order, but it can also be a blast.

What You Get: This will vary significantly depending on the program, but here are a few examples: Trek America combines sightseeing with adventure on road trips across America. Group leaders make a base pay of $1,150/month. Visions Service Adventures, with programs from Alaska to Australia that combine community service with outdoor adventure, offers stipends starting at $250/week, plus housing, meals, and travel expenses. Snowboard the Swiss Alps with youth who sign up with West Coast Connection, and make $100 to $400/week, plus basic living expenses.

What It Costs: Nothing for most programs, unless you need to invest in trip-specific necessities such as a backpack, sleeping bag, or an updated passport.

What You Need: Requirements are different for each program, but in general you'll have a better chance of landing a leadership role if you are experienced in travel, have some knowledge of the area of focus (e.g., if you're leading a scuba diving adventure, a background in marine biology will serve you well), are charismatic, responsible, intelligent, and physically capable of fully participating in the activities of the trip. Other requirements might include CPR certification or first aid skills, fluency in the language of your destination, or experience in previous group leadership positions.

Perks

• You will meet other adventurous, fun, and interesting people, and experience the thrill of travel yourself.

• Most programs cover virtually all of your expenses, so you should be able to save the majority of your earnings.

Downsides

• Not every group will be a pleasure to spend every minute of every day with. Years ago my mother led a bicycle trip across Europe. Though she doesn't regret the experience (she met my father in training, after all), she spent a great deal of the trip chasing around teenagers who preferred to go out and get drunk rather than sleep at night.

<u>Sites to Check Out</u>
- **www.backdoorjobs.com** has extensive listings of adventure trips that hire leaders on a regular basis.

- **www.lookingforadventure.com** has links by category (biking, rafting, cruises, etc.). Not all of the companies or programs represented are actively looking for staff, but if you find one that piques your interest, it doesn't hurt to contact them and let them know you'd love to be part of their team.

- **www.oapn.net**—This site is just job listings from members of the Outdoor Adventure Professional Network.

61. Resort Receptionist

<u>What You Do:</u> You will check people in and out of their rooms, answer the phone, and accommodate special requests (room changes, switching departure dates, or getting somebody to bring a toothbrush or an ironing board to the guest's suite). What makes this different than any other front desk job? You'll be at a luxurious resort, surrounded by beaches and palm trees or snow-covered ski slopes, swimming pools, spas, and elegant dining rooms.

<u>What You Get:</u> $5.15 to $10/hour. In addition, many resorts offer free room and board for their employees.

<u>What It Costs:</u> Nothing, except maybe a ticket to get to your new job.

<u>What You Need:</u> It's helpful to have customer service skills, be fluent in English (if you speak other languages besides, this will definitely be to your advantage), and to have ample patience for difficult guests.

<u>Perks</u>
• Most resorts give their employees access to all the facilities—sauna, pool, exercise equipment, etc.

• Though you'll be working most of the time, you should also have opportunities to enjoy the surroundings.

• It's easy to save money when all your necessities are provided for and your free time is limited.

<u>Downsides</u>
• Even your "off" time can seem like work, since staff is often expected to present a positive image when they're around guests, whether they're on the clock or not.

<u>Sites to Check Out</u>
• **www.jobmonkey.com/resorts/html/front_desk.html** includes a good description of life working at a resort, as well as job listings.

• **www.resortjobs.com** has job listings for resorts across the U.S.

• **www.hospitalityonline.com**—You can find some resort job listings here as well, though it also includes "regular" hotel jobs.

62. Work on a Cruise Ship

<u>What You Do:</u> There are dozens of different kinds of jobs to be done on cruise ships—they're basically floating cities, and it takes all sorts to run a city. Positions that don't require any unusual skills include waitstaff, bar staff, administrative assistants, cabin stewards/stewardesses (housekeepers), casino dealers, dishwashers, laundry staff, locker attendants, pool attendants, and receptionists. If you have particular skills in the entertainment, beauty, fitness, or culinary fields, you'll be in even higher demand.

<u>What You Get:</u> $1,200 to $2,500/month for most labor positions, or $3,000 to $4,500/month for jobs that require unusual talent or skill, plus room and board.

<u>What It Costs:</u> Nothing. Well, you might have to buy a uniform. But some cruise lines will even pay for your transportation to and from the port, which more than makes up for what you'll spend on a white-collared shirt and black vest.

<u>What You Need:</u> Not much, for the majority of jobs, although it is helpful if you speak more than one language (including English), and if you've had prior experience in the area of employment you're applying for.

Perks
- You will get to see ports all over the world (or at least all over wherever your ship is sailing).

- On your time off, you will probably get to enjoy many of the luxuries the passengers do, such as good food, spas, pools, exercise equipment, and, if you make the right friends, massages.

- Free laundry

- Health insurance, depending on your contract

Downsides
- Living arrangements are often cramped and lack privacy (think first year in a college dorm).

- Seasickness

- You usually have to commit to working for three to four months, which can feel like a long time when you're on a boat, especially if you don't bond well with the rest of the crew.

- Working seven days a week is not uncommon on cruise ships.

Sites to Check Out
- **www.cruiseshipjob.net**—I don't recommend that you pay the $59 application fee (at least not until you've thoroughly researched free options for applying to positions), but this site will give you a good idea of what jobs are available and how much they pay.

- **www.carnival.com**—Follow the link for "fun jobs" to see what positions are open.

- **www.intrav.com**—Look for the "employment" link.

- **www.princess.com**—Click on "jobs."

TIPS

- There is a lot of turnover in cruise ship employment, but there is also a fair amount of competition. Cruise lines sometimes receive thousands of applications a week. Be sure your application is neat, specific (apply for a particular position—don't just say you're looking for work) and includes a resume with any relevant experience, and be sure you address it to the person responsible for receiving applications in your field.

- There are a lot of Web sites that "guarantee" job placement if you spend $50 or so to become a member. Some of these may work, but many are scams. Search through all the free informational sites before you resort to spending any cash.

63. Kayak Tour Guide off San Juan Island

<u>What You Do:</u> Besides teaching passengers the basics of sea kayaking and water safety, you will also be a "boat naturalist," educating passengers about whales, birds, and general ecology on a three- or five-hour tour. You'll be first mate, too, accountable to the captain, giving attention to passengers and their needs (providing blankets, jackets, binoculars, etc.), and cleaning and preparing vessels before and after trips.

<u>What You Get:</u> Up to $12/hour, plus tips

<u>What It Costs:</u> Staff usually rent houses together on the island, three to five per house, at about $250 to $300 a month per person. You'll need that much saved for the first month's rent (plus enough for food), but after that you should be making more than enough to break even.

<u>What You Need:</u> CPR Certification, ability to lift 50 pounds, and a good attitude. A background in natural sciences is preferable, and you have to be at least 21.

<u>Perks</u>
• Discounts on outdoor gear and at the local restaurant

• Discounts on kayak and whale watching tours for family and friends

• Hang out and explore on the "jewels of the Pacific Northwest," Puget Sound's San Juan Islands.

<u>Downsides</u>
• You'll be working 50-hour weeks.

• There's a dress code. (But it's really not bad—T-shirt with company logo, khakis, baseball cap. You can handle it.)

<u>Sites to Check Out</u>
• **www.sanjuansafaris.com/jobs.html**—San Juan Safaris offers sea kayaking and whale-watching boat tours of Washington's beautiful San Juan Islands. They hire guides only for the summer months.

- **www.guidetosanjuans.com**—An introduction to the San Juan Islands (note that San Juan Island is one of a group of islands, collectively called the San Juan Islands).

- **http://whale.wheelock.edu**—If you want to boost your marine life knowledge before applying, study this site.

64. Commercial Skydiving in New Zealand

<u>What You Do:</u> First you'll have to get a license, which you can do at the New Zealand Skydiving School in Christ Church or Pudding Hill, New Zealand, in a course that takes 32 weeks and includes 200 jumps. The program is divided into five modules, beginning with 25 skydives to build your experience and confidence. After that you'll study dropzone operations, and then learn how to video while diving and develop workforce promotion and self-management skills. The final 12 weeks you'll spend working in a commercial dropzone, which will hopefully lead to paid employment as a freefall camera man, as a parachute packer, or in manifesting (coordinating the day-to-day activities of a dropzone).

<u>What You Get:</u> Around $30,000/year for freefall camera work, or $9 to $15/hour for parachute packing or manifesting.

<u>What It Costs:</u> The course is the equivalent of about $10,000.

<u>What You Need:</u> No fear of heights, or at least a willingness to get over it fast.

<u>Perks</u>
• This job will definitely give you bragging rights.

• The New Zealand Skydiving School boasts a 98 percent employment rate for its students.

• New Zealand has been called "The Adventure Capital of the World"—not to mention that it is also one of the most stunningly beautiful places you'll ever see.

• You have a really good chance of living through training, at least. According to one source, only one out of 64,091 skydiving jumps result in death.

<u>Downsides</u>
• If at first you don't succeed . . . you're dead. (Or at least permanently maimed—but probably dead.)

<u>Sites to Check Out</u>
• **www.nzskydivingschool.com**—The New Zealand School of Sky Diving

• **www.dropzone.com**—Lots of good articles, classifieds, news, and links

• **www.afn.org/skydive**—All sorts of related links

65. FEMA Disaster Assistance Employee

<u>What You Do:</u> As one of approximately 4,000 FEMA reservists, you will be on-call for a certain number of months out of the year, meaning that if an emergency occurs and your services are needed during those months, you have to be willing to drop everything, fly to the emergency site, and be prepared to stay for a minimum of two to six weeks. At the site, you may be assigned to any of several responsibilities, including assessing the individual financial needs of victims and guiding them through the aid application process, administrative or technical work, or other program coordination efforts. You will likely be working in a temporary makeshift "office" (which could very well be a tent), set up as part of the emergency response. Chances are you will not be directly involved in search and rescue, rebuilding, or other physical labor, but you should be willing to help wherever you are needed.

<u>What You Get:</u> Pay will vary according to the work you do and the site you are at. You will be provided with travel expenses to and from the site, accommodations, a food stipend, and an hourly or per diem wage. Hourly wages rage from $9 to $35/hour and almost always include additional pay for overtime if you work more than an eight-hour shift.

<u>What It Costs:</u> Nothing

<u>What You Need:</u> Some DAE positions have very minimal requirements, the most demanding of which is that you have to be able to leave home and travel to an emergency site at a day or two's notice. Other positions require specific skill sets or experi-

ence, such as computer proficiency or other technical knowledge. Regardless of your responsibilities, you should be able to work responsibly with little supervision under stressful circumstances and sometimes for long hours.

Perks

• Get back some of your tax dollars and help people at the same time!

• FEMA employees are generally put up in very comfortable—even luxurious—accommodations, assuming that all such housing hasn't been swept away by wind or floods, or whatever the disaster. (Lavish accommodations are a great perk if you're a FEMA employee—if you're a taxpayer of any other occupation, this is a little disturbing.)

Downsides

• Being on call can make it difficult to commit to other plans or employment opportunities. And FEMA won't pay you unless you're actually working.

• Being in a disaster zone can take its toll on you physically, mentally, and emotionally.

• FEMA's gotten a pretty bad rap ever since Katrina. If you tell someone you work for FEMA, don't expect to see that same gleam of respect and admiration in their eyes that you once might have.

Sites to Check Out

• **www.fema.gov/plan/ehp/employment.shtm**—Here's the official job description. You should look around the rest of the FEMA site as well to better familiarize yourself with the organization before you apply.

66. Dog Handler in Alaska

<u>What You Do:</u> Ride on a custom-made wheeled dog sled pulled by Alaskan huskies; assist the musher, who will also be acting as tour guide for guests paying for sledding tours; and help with feeding, cleaning, grooming, and various other duties.

<u>What You Get:</u> $12 to $15/hour, plus performance-based incentives

<u>What It Costs:</u> Whatever it costs to get you to Skagway, Alaska

<u>What You Need:</u> You must be good with dogs and with people, be physically fit, motivated, and work well with a team.

<u>Perks</u>
• This is a seasonal position (May through September), which is enough time to enjoy the natural beauty of Alaska without going crazy from civilization deprivation.

• You can horseback ride and explore the Klondike Gold Rush National Park on your time off.

<u>Downsides</u>
• There is a lot of manual labor involved, which can be exhausting.

• Chances are you won't just be working with the dogs. Be prepared to deal with tourists and be willing to do paperwork, maintenance, or other miscellaneous chores to help keep things running smoothly.

<u>Sites to Check Out</u>
- **www.alaskaexcursions.com**—The company you will be working for.

- **www.skagway.com**—The town you'll be working in.

- **www.nps.gov/klgo**—The park you'll be riding through.

67. Harvester in Australia

<u>What You Do:</u> Hand pick, prune, or pack one of Australia's many crops. Around harvesting time, local farmers have a difficult time finding enough help, so they are eager to hire "outsiders" looking for some cash and a new experience. Crops include berries, apples, citrus fruit, mangoes, bananas, grapes, tomatoes, and cotton. The produce is placed into buckets, lugs, or baskets and carried back to packing sheds, canneries, or other processing facilities. There are also opportunities for wool harvesters and flower cutters.

<u>What You Get:</u> Wages may be offered on a weekly basis, on a piecework basis (the more you pick the more you get), or by the hour. However it comes, it works out to about $10 to $15/hour. Days are long, generally starting early in the morning and at times going well past dark, and work is often six days a week, with Saturday being the day off to accommodate market requirements. Some farms offer free

room and board, or they may take out a reasonable portion of your wages to cover living costs.

<u>What It Costs:</u> Besides paying for a flight to Australia, you should have a few hundred dollars in reserve. If weather does not cooperate, sometimes there's no work for a day, a week, or longer.

<u>What You Need:</u> This is physical work, and, though you don't have to be Hulk Hogan, you should be able to climb ladders, carry heavy buckets, and withstand hot conditions. In addition, you will need a work visa (unless you're Australian), which can be obtained by following the instructions found at **www.dimia.gov.au**.

<u>Perks</u>
- Harvesting is a great way to see Australia without draining the bank account.

- There are crops throughout the year in different regions, making it possible to work your way through virtually the whole continent.

<u>Downsides</u>
- Weather has a way of messing with your plans. Be sure to check with local offices and farmers before going to be sure the crops are on the same schedule you are.

- Without transportation it can be difficult to get to and from the farm. Possible solutions are to buy a cheap used car when you arrive and have fun driving on the left side of the road, try to find close accommodations, or ask ahead of time if you can set up a tent somewhere nearby.

- Picking wages in any country are pretty much the lowest of any job available.

Sites to Check Out
- **www.jobsearch.gov.au/harvesttrail**—Follow the links to the National Harvest Trail Guide, and read the whole thing.

- **www.waywardbus.com.au/seaswork.html** has a list of potential employers.

TIPS

- Don't forget your sunscreen and "sunnies" (sunglasses)!

- Tote some insect repellent along, too.

- Wear sturdy shoes.

68. English Teacher Abroad

<u>What You Do:</u> The simplest way to teach English in a foreign country is to go via a certified program, which usually requires you to take a class (through correspondence or at a school) before they set you up with a job teaching English, hopefully in the country of your choice. There is a particular need for English teachers in Asia, so if an Asian country is your top choice, you're in luck.

<u>What You Get:</u> This varies according to the country and program, but there are offers out there for up to $1,000/week, plus benefits and even a place to live.

<u>What It Costs:</u> For a basic certification program (generally about 60 hours) with job placement, expect to pay from $300 to $1,000. Some agencies require you to pay airfare to your destination and then reimburse you upon arrival. Others will cover your tickets up front.

<u>What You Need:</u> You'll need at least a high school diploma, and sometimes a BA or BS. You'll also need to get some sort of TESL/TEFL certificate, but, as mentioned, many programs set you up with certificate programs prior to sending you abroad. You should be fluent in English, and some programs require a U.S. passport.

<u>Perks</u>
• Teaching abroad is an amazing opportunity to delve into another culture while earning a substantial income.

<u>Downsides</u>
• For some people, living alone in a foreign country proves to be a very lonely experience, especially if they don't speak the language. However, many teachers get involved in groups and activities almost right away and find that being so immersed in a culture develops their language skills very rapidly.

<u>Sites to Check Out</u>
• **www.englishfirst.com** is one of the most up-front sites for TESL/TEFL programs that I've seen. It tells you how much you'll make, what the accommodations will be—even who to contact for local prices on tampons (seriously). EF doesn't provide TESL training, however. They recommend that you go through a certificate program before applying.

• **www.transitionsabroad.com/listings/work/esl/ bestwebsites.shtml** has links to the best Web sites for teaching English abroad.

• **www.americantesol.com**—The American TESOL Institute offers training online or in class.

LINGO

• TESL = Teaching English as a Second Language (to students who live in an English-speaking country, such as the U.S. or England)

• TEFL = Teaching English as a Foreign Language (to students living in non-English-speaking countries)

---

69. Snowmaker

<u>What You Do:</u> Ride a snowmobile around the ski slopes, setting up and tearing down, hooking and unhooking, and repairing snowmaking equipment.

<u>What You Get:</u> $8 to $10/hour

<u>What It Costs:</u> Nothing

<u>What You Need:</u> You have to be reasonably strong, not mind being outside in the cold, and able to work night shifts.

<u>Perks</u>
• You get to zoom around the mountain on a snowmobile all day (or night).

• You might get a season pass and/or discounts at the ski/snowboard shop.

<u>Downsides</u>
• Much of the snowmaking is done overnight, which means you'll probably have to be out at the coldest part of the night during the coldest days in the year.

<u>Sites to Check Out</u>
• **www.snowmasters.com**—Get a head-start by familiarizing yourself with snowmaking equipment.

• **www.coolworks.com/ski-resort-jobs**—Find links to employment opportunities at ski resorts all over the U.S.

• **www.natives.co.uk** includes ski-related jobs all over the world.

• **www.skiingthenet.com** has more jobs listings.

Chapter Six

CAPITALIST PURSUITS

Marketing, Selling Things, and Letting Your Body Work for You

Body Part Model

Call Room Operator
Focus Groups
Soap Maker
Sandwich Board Advertising
Liquor or Beer Promoter
Gift Baskets
Home-Based Sales Representative
Promotional Model
Face-to-Face Fundraiser
Political Pin Sales
Sperm Donor
Egg Donor
Body Part Model
Hair Sales
Plasma Sales
Medical or Psychological Study
Participant
Body Advertising

Art is making something out of nothing and selling it.

—Frank Zappa

The Tooth Fairy teaches children that they can sell body parts for money.

—David Richerby

PROXY PRANK

The walls of the cubicle were gray with flecks of tan, and I was surprised to realize that it was a burlap-like material that covered the three flimsy walls that made up my cell. Was that for decorative purposes, was it meant to give a sense of ease and comfort that bare walls could not? Or was it to help muffle the steady chorus of voices resounding from every angle, like crickets clacking away long into the night? I tapped a knuckle gently against the wall on my right, trying to determine what was beneath the textured, rough fabric. Not sharp like metal, or solid as wood. Was I sitting in a *plastic* box, masked by cheap upholstery and glowing with dull fluorescent lighting?

I began to twist back and forth in the black office chair, waiting for the next call to connect through the headset strapped over my ears. Any moment there would be a beep and the computer screen would prompt me with a name. A stranger from somewhere in the Midwest would greet me and I'd begin the script with as sweet and professional a voice as I could muster: "Good evening, Mr. Jones. My name is Abigail Gehring and I'm calling regarding your current investment with the Lexicon Slow Growth Fund. I wanted to confirm that you received the proxy material for the upcoming shareholder's meeting. Did you receive that?"

The words had fallen from my lips so many times they had begun to lose their meaning. Often I repeated that portion of the script three or four times over before whoever was on the other end of the line figured out what the heck I was talking about. "What now? What are you selling?"

"No, Ma'am," (with a polite laugh) "I'm not selling anything. I'm calling regarding your Lexicon Slow Growth fund."

Then, after a brief confused pause, I'd hear a muffled yell, "Honey? Do we have a growth fund? Somebody here's asking about a Leprechaun somethin' or other. Here. You talk to her."

"Hello?" A man's voice now, a little gruff and already annoyed.

"Hello, Mr. Jones? My name is Abigail and I'm calling regarding your Lexicon Slow Growth Fund. It's part of your IRA rollover? I wanted to confirm that you received . . ."

And so on. Sometimes I'd get to explain what the board was proposing for that particular fund (I don't think one person I spoke to had actually read the proxy material. Who would?) and occasionally I could get someone to vote. More often they'd hang up with an icy "not interested," still unconvinced I wasn't trying to scam them into purchasing diet pills or an overpriced vacuum or something. I'd click the box labeled "Not interested," knowing that it meant they'd be called again every couple of days until they finally gave in to being "interested" enough to vote, just to get us off their backs.

My second week there, the automatic dialer began to malfunction, which is right about the time I began to realize maybe proxy calling was not for me. The same homes were called repeatedly every few minutes, over and over, until the shareholders became so livid that I worked in a perpetual cringe, shoulders tensing into rocks while litanies of curses traveled thousands of miles of phone wires to reach me. Some of my coworkers seemed able to laugh it off or turn the calls into scandalous stories to share between calls—"You'll never believe what that woman just said to me! Lord, did she have a mouth!" I guess that worked for me at first, too, until the steady influx of insults began to wear on my psyche, and it was all I could do not to burst into tears, even as the captain waltzed up and down the hall behind me, calling his inspirational mantra: "Courtesy, enthusiasm, speed!"

I lasted less than two weeks. I simply wasn't motivated by the promise that if I worked really hard (at sitting there, I guess) and became one of the company's top callers (which was totally subjective, since the system that counted outgoing calls was, I'm convinced, a list of randomly generated numbers), I could have my very own cubicle. Though a few eager beavers seemed to really aspire to a whole gray plastic box to themselves, to me it was not even vaguely appealing. The best few days of the job had been the first ones, when I had Victor sharing my cell, a big black dude who chatted with old ladies from the South about the weather for long relaxed minutes before ever broaching the subject of stocks, a practice strictly against policy and endlessly amusing. Sometimes we'd play tick-tack-toe or dot-to-dot between calls, and a few times we managed to get into fairly deep conversations about religion or relationships, despite being interrupted every time one of us got a beep and had to take a call. Even when we were both so bored we had absolutely nothing to say, it helped to know someone was sharing my mind numbing agony. When he stopped showing up for work, the cubicle felt much too large and isolating. The last thing I wanted was to be stuck by myself for the rest of my proxy-calling career.

Probably the best story I got to share with Victor before he had the good sense to quit came late one night, as the dialer plagued the Western states at just about their dinner time, a few zones earlier than our New Jersey office. I found myself trying to talk to a young-ish sounding man with a slight Chicago accent (a barely perceptible lengthening of certain vowels and clipping of others). There were children in the background who seemed to be commanding most of his attention. I imagined two boys and a girl, alternately squabbling and begging their dad for judicial interference.

"Would you like me to call you back later?" I offered.

"No, no. Who did you say you are?"

I began my spiel again, pausing intermittently to allow for the conversations he was also having with the kids. Things were getting rowdier by the second, voices escalating rapidly. He insisted that I stay on the line—that he really wanted to vote—despite my repeated suggestions to call at a better time. So I waited patiently, re-explaining the issues to be voted on several times and holding while he tried to regain control of the mounting chaos, which sounded from my end like a bad recording of an old war movie.

Suddenly there was a loud crash. And then silence.

I waited a moment, listening. "Hello? Are you okay?"

Scratching and rustling occupied close to a minute, and then I heard a shaky voice—"Hi. Uh, yeah. The kids just knocked me down the stairs."

"Are you okay, sir?"

"Yeah. No. What's the number for rescue?"

"911. Call 911." My voice was steady but urgent. "I'm going to let you go now."

"No, no! I want to vote. Tell me again what my choices are?"

"Um, okay . . ." I scanned my prompts, collecting myself. As I started to go over the material with him again, in an abbreviated form, he interrupted, breathless.

"What's the number for 911?"

Ever since that day I've been waiting for the perfect opportunity to try this on some other bored telemarketer. It could be the highlight of their career. In fact, if you're interrupted by a sales call while reading this section on promotions, marketing, and how to use your body—legally—to make money, you might also give it a try. I imagine it could be quite amusing.

70. Call Room Operator

<u>What You Do:</u> There are many different kinds of phone jobs out there. Here are two common ones:

- **Proxy calling** is phoning individuals to get them to vote or offer their opinion on a particular subject. For example, when corporations are considering a merge or any sort of significant change, sometimes they are required to get a certain number of votes from their shareholders. You get to call them up, explain the issue on the table, and ask them if they'd like to vote. No real persuasive powers are required, as the goal is to get them to vote, not to sway their opinion in any way.

- **Phone solicitation** requires a little more assertiveness. It's your job to get people to buy a product, service, or donate money to a cause.

<u>What You Get:</u> $8 to $20/hour. Solicitation jobs may be commission-based, so if you're really good you can make more.

<u>What You Need:</u> Confidence speaking on the phone and willingness to put up with the flack you will inevitably get from people who had their dinner interrupted by your call.

<u>Perks</u>
- If you like to talk on the phone, here's your chance.

- Late night or early morning shifts are often available since people in other time zones may need to be called. I was a proxy caller for a short while so I could be at dance rehearsals during the day and work from mid-afternoon until 11pm.

Downsides
• People will hate you and they won't hesitate to tell you so. Even if you're not trying to sell something, they will assume you are. And if you *are* trying to sell something—well, good luck. Some people are really good at it and genuinely enjoy it. Most people are ready to wrap the phone cord around their neck by the end of a week.

Sites to Check Out
• **www.craigslist.com** often posts call room jobs

• **www.callcentercareers.com** offers more job listings.

71. Focus Groups

What You Do: Meet with a group (generally 6 to 10 other people) led by a moderator to give your opinion on an idea, evaluate a service, or test a product. Focus groups are a way for companies to gain valuable qualitative data on what and how consumers think.

What You Get: $40 to $100/hour. Focus groups generally last 1 to 2 hours.

What It Costs: Nothing

What You Need: Requirements vary according to the session. If you sign up with a focus group agency, you will probably have to supply information about yourself (education, profession, marital status, etc.)

and then they will call you when they have a study for which you might be a good match. If there are more specific qualifications (e.g., you must own an mp3 player, or eat primarily organic produce) they will ask you about your suitability before inviting you to participate in that particular group.

Perks
- Free stuff! Oftentimes you'll get samples of whatever product is being discussed.

- A lot of companies will hand you your pay in cash as you walk out the door.

- Very flexible—when a company invites you to participate you are under no obligation to do so.

Downsides
- You can't count on focus groups as a steady income. Many companies only allow you to participate in a focus group once every six months.

Sites to Check Out
Sign up with one or several of the following companies:

- **www.focusroom.com**
- **www.greatopinions.com**
- **www.shugollresearch.com**
- **www.focusgroup.com**
- **www.iopinion.com**

TIP

Be wary of Internet sites that require you to pay a fee for access to a list of focus group recruiters. There are plenty of companies you can sign up with directly for free.

72. Soap Maker

<u>What You Do:</u> Making soap can be as easy as buying a bar of soap, melting it, and pouring it into a new mould to harden. But to make a greater profit and gain a good reputation as a soap craftsperson, you're better off learning the process of mixing lye, fat, water, and fragrances to create your own unique sudsy bars. As long as people get dirty, there will be a market for soap. The problem is that because you can buy a cheap bar of mass-produced soap at the drug store, why would anyone want to spend three times as much on your handmade soap? Answer: Because your soap feels nicer, looks prettier, is sweeter smelling, or has some other unique quality to it.

<u>What You Get:</u> A medium-sized bar of handmade soap can go for up to $8 at a nice boutique in a ritzy area. You can expect to get $1 net profit for every $5 in sales.

<u>What It Costs:</u> $100 or so: $25 to $50 for an accurate kitchen scale; $20 for a stick blender (like you'd use for a milkshake—this will make your life much easier and cut your work time down significantly); and $40 to $50 for enough ingredients to make about 95 bars (about 45 cents per bar). If you buy the ingredients in bulk, your price per bar will go down, but I wouldn't make a batch any bigger than this for your first attempt—sometimes it takes a try or two to get it just right, and this will be enough to allow you to keep several for yourself and to put a small basket of bars in a few boutiques.

What You Need:
• Patience (from start to suds, the process takes about a month—granted, most of that time the stuff is just sitting on your counter chilling, but still).

• Ability to follow a recipe carefully (if the last cake mix you tried to bake turned into something resembling a plastic Frisbee, this might not be the job for you).

• Enough space to store the soap while it's setting.

Perks
• This is a fun, creative process. When you get good at it, you can teach others how to do it and charge for the lessons.

Downsides
• If you forget to wear gloves, or if you spill the lye, you can end up with some crazy burns.

• Occasionally something inexplicable goes wrong and you end up with a bad batch, and all your work is for naught.

Sites to Check Out
• **www.teachsoap.com**—This is a wonderful site with recipes, tips, and detailed information on costs to help you calculate how much to charge.

• **www.goplanetearth.com**—All the supplies you'll need.

• **www.thesage.com/calcs/lyecalc2.php**—If, after you've gotten the hang of things, you decide to experiment with your own recipes a bit, this calculator will help you determine how much lye you need in proportion to the other ingredients.

73. Sandwich Board Advertising

<u>What You Do:</u> Stand on the sidewalk of busy metropolitan areas handing out flyers with a sign hanging over your chest like a big smock. Sandwich boards are one of the oldest forms of advertisement, and they're still a very popular method of attracting pedestrians to restaurants or other business that are tucked around the corner from the busiest pedestrian flow.

<u>What You Get:</u> $7 to $9/hour

<u>What It Costs:</u> Nothing

<u>What You Need:</u> Ability to stand around for long hours (if you have foot problems, this is not the job for you).

<u>Perks</u>
• You can move around as you wish, getting some decent exercise, as long as you stay in the general prescribed vicinity.

<u>Downsides</u>
• In cold or wet weather, there's really no avoiding being cold and wet.

Sites to Check Out
• **www.craigslist.com** often lists sandwich board
job openings.

HOW DO YOU GET THE JOB?

The best way to get a sandwich board job is to find a sandwich board advertiser on the street and inquire at the store he or she is representing. There's a good possibility they will need someone to fill in certain shifts that their current advertiser can't cover. Alternately, you can march into any store and ask if they hire sandwich board advertisers. For whatever reason, men's suits retailers frequently advertise in this way and are good places to check.

74. Liquor or Beer Promoter

What You Do: Hang out at a bar, make small talk with strangers, and try to get people to buy whatever liquor you're promoting. You'll probably have some cool stuff to hand out, like key chains, T-shirts, visors, or glow in the dark leis. In some states you can give away the liquor or beer itself or buy people shots on the company account. You may need to keep records of how much liquor was sold and report it back to the company.

What You Get: $20 to $35/hour. Shifts usually last two hours, anytime between 6 PM and 2 AM.

<u>What It Costs:</u> Nothing

<u>What You Need:</u> Must be at least 21, attractive, and friendly. You should be comfortable approaching male and female customers, whether they're alone at the bar or clumped in a tight group.

Perks

- In an effort to avoid boring nights at slow bars, I've started inviting my friends to meet me wherever I am working. That way, once I've made the rounds, I can "promote" to folks I actually want to hang out with. Of course, you don't want to make it too obvious, and you shouldn't totally ignore the rest of the guests, but with a little tact it can make for a fun and profitable evening. I mean really, who doesn't want to get paid to chill with their friends at a bar?

Downsides

- You're not allowed to drink on the job. (This rule is routinely broken, but I wouldn't recommend it. Oftentimes the bartender or manager is expected to double as a spy, reporting back to the company on the quality of the promotion. If you get busted, there's a good chance your promo days will be over.)

- Prepare to be hit on.

- For me, the worst part of the job is trying to yell over loud music. I always leave feeling like I've swallowed a piece of eighty-grit sandpaper.

Sites to Check Out

• **www.craigslist.com** regularly lists liquor promotional jobs under "marketing jobs." As a rule, most liquor companies don't provide information on becoming a model through their Web sites, so looking through general job listings is the way to go.

• **www.jager.com**—Every rule has its exception, and Jagermeister is it in this case. Click on "Connecting" and then "Jagerettes and Jager Dudes." Jagermeister also gives out some of the coolest promotional freebies I've seen.

75. Gift Baskets

<u>What You Do:</u> Put together baskets of nice "gifty" items, such as non-perishable gourmet food products (jams and jellies, fancy crackers, chocolates, dipping oil); gardening supplies (gloves, spade, soap and lotion for treating tired hands); beauty products (lotions, sprays, nail polish, loofah); or kitchen items (wooden spoon, potholder, dish towel, cork screw). Sell the baskets to boutiques, or customize baskets according to a customer's orders.

<u>What You Get:</u> This depends on what you put in the basket. Usually you can put a 100 percent markup on the items you purchase, so if you spend $30, you can sell the basket for $60.

<u>What It Costs:</u> Again, this varies a lot. The tricky part is purchasing items that are inexpensive enough that you can mark up the price and still find a buyer. This may sound cheap, but you can get

some pretty nice things from a good dollar store, flea market, or discount department store. Buying wholesale is an option, too.

<u>What You Need:</u> You'll need good taste, a feel for what will sell, and the ability to present it in an appealing package.

<u>Perks</u>
• Picking out nice things and arranging them artfully can be really fun.

<u>Downsides</u>
• You'll be surprised how quickly little knickknacks add up in price. Give yourself a budget for each basket so you know you can still sell the finished product at a reasonable price and make a profit.

<u>Sites to Check Out</u>
• **www.powerhomebiz.com/vol100/giftbasket. htm**—This is an excellent article on starting a gift basket business.

• **www.gifttree.com**—Browse this site and the one below for inspiration

• **www.giftbaskets.com**

76. Home-Based Sales Representative

<u>What You Do:</u> Sell a product (beauty, health, and kitchen products are popular categories) for a company to friends, family, or anyone you can get interested. Sometimes this involves holding parties in

your home, giving demonstrations, offering free "beauty consultations," going door-to-door, or any number of other marketing techniques to get people to want (or feel obligated to buy) your product.

<u>What You Get:</u> $0 to $200,000+/year. This HUGE range is because most companies offer incentive-based salaries, meaning that if you don't sell anything, you won't make anything. However, if you're really into it and if you have access to the sort of people who will want your product (keep in mind that expensive makeup will not sell well to an impoverished farming community, for example), then there is a lot of earning potential. Most companies advertise that there is no limit to your earnings, and this is true, as far as the company is concerned—after all, they're making money off of what you sell, too—but, depending on your situation, there may be a limit to the number of people you can get to actually shell out money for what you're offering.

<u>What It Costs:</u> Some companies require you to buy a certain amount of the product at a wholesale price and then sell it at a profit (Mary Kay, a cosmetics company, requires you to buy a minimum of $100 to begin, but it's 90 percent refundable if you don't end up selling the stuff). Others require you to become a member before you can buy or sell anything (the fee to become a member of Shaklee, a natural health supplement company, is $19.95).

<u>What You Need:</u> It will definitely help if you are an enthusiastic go-getter type with a knack for sales. But if not, probably no one will stop you from trying.

Perks
- You really are your own boss. You set your own hours, market where you want, to whom you want, and keep track of your own inventory.

- Many of these companies do offer high quality products, which you can get for yourself as well as to sell, at wholesale prices.

- Some companies offer extra bonuses, like cars or vacations, for top sellers.

Downsides
- You are not guaranteed an income based on how many hours you put in.

- The prices that you have to sell the products at in order to make a profit are generally rather exorbitant, at least compared to similar products offered at department stores.

Sites to Check Out
- The following are all companies worth looking into: **www.shaklee.com**, **www.avon.com**, **www.melaleuca.com**, **www.tupperware.com**, **www.cutco.com**, **www.marykay.com**.

77. Promotional Model

What You Do: Attract attention to a product or service by standing around looking hot. Oh, and talking about the product, answering questions, handing out flyers, etc.—but mostly looking hot. Promotional models are recruited for boat and car shows, concerts, sporting events, gaming conventions, and malls.

<u>What You Get:</u> $15 to $25/hour. Promotions may last from a couple of hours to full eight-hour days.

<u>What It Costs:</u> Nothing. Beware of agencies that require you to pay a fee for their services. There are plenty of promotional/marketing companies you can sign up with directly, free of charge.

<u>What You Need:</u> You must be attractive, both physically and in personality. You should be outgoing, confident, fun, and be able to act in a professional manner. Also, being able to speak clearly is a definite plus. And sometimes knowledge of a particular product (e.g., computers or video games) may work to your advantage.

<u>Perks</u>

• Unlike a lot of modeling gigs, you don't have to look like an emaciated giraffe to be a promo model. Companies are seeking men and women who look naturally attractive, who are vibrant, healthy, and personable—not like the typical runway models.

• Many promotional modeling agencies have ties to the pageant scene, which could be your break if that's an area you'd like to get into.

<u>Downsides</u>

• Some days you just don't want to smile, but you have to—it's your job.

• Certain assignments require costumes, which have the potential to be a definite downside.

• You won't make as much as print or runway models.

Links to Check Out
- **www.promomodels.com** is a nationwide staffing agency for event marketing and promotions.

- **www.kandu-marketing.com** is full of marketing and promotional resources.

- **www.lifeofamodel.com/promotional_model. html**—This article has some good advice for new promo models.

78. Face-to-Face Fundraiser

<u>What You Do:</u> Stand in well-trafficked areas and talk to passersby about whatever organization you are representing. Try to get people to contribute to your cause by giving a one-time donation or committing to sending money on a regular basis.

<u>What You Get:</u> You should get an hourly wage, in addition to commission-based profits or "performance-related-pay," meaning if you're doing well, your hourly wages will go up. Expect to average $350 to $550/week for full time employment, though more is certainly possible.

<u>What It Costs:</u> Nothing

<u>What You Need:</u> Most companies don't have any formal requirements, but you should be outgoing, friendly, persistent, and a good verbal communicator. Also, these jobs are primarily available in urban areas, so if you live in the sticks, you're probably out of luck.

Perks
• Some companies offer traveling positions, which allow you to tour various cities with a team of fundraisers. Travel expenses and accommodations are generally provided.

• You can work for an organization you really believe in, knowing that on some level the job you're doing is making the world a better place.

Downsides
• You'll get snubbed most of the time. People are busy and they don't want to stop and chat and be made to feel guilty if they don't fork over some cash.

• People *really* don't want to stop and chat if it's raining, very cold, or particularly windy. But you have to stay out there anyway.

Sites to Check Out
• **www.dialoguejobs.com**—Work for this company and raise money for Children's International, Greenpeace, Amnesty International, WWF, and CARE International

• **www.jobsthatmatter.org** focuses their fundraising on social and environmental issues.

79. Political Pin Sales

<u>What You Do:</u> Request pins or other memorabilia from political party headquarters or local representatives, and sell them. You can go door-to-door, stand on the street, or even post them on eBay.

<u>What You Get:</u> $1 to $2 per pin

<u>What It Costs</u> Nothing! That's the great thing about this—political parties give away all sorts of free stuff. Ask and you shall receive! If only politics was always that simple . . .

<u>What You Need:</u> A good salesperson is friendly, a little bit aggressive (but not pushy), and is a highly skilled sweet talker. Your goal is to make the buyer feel like she is fulfilling her patriotic duty by purchasing one of your official party pins (even if she's mostly just filling your pocket). Of course, there's no need to lie—sporting a pin may very well influence other voters. If it didn't, probably the political parties would have quit shelling them out by now. The point is, even if you remember more about the ninth-grade biology class you failed than what the candidates stand for, if you pretend you really believe in the power of pins, you'll make some sales.

<u>Perks</u>
• This is something you can do at the drop of a hat, anytime, anywhere. Always carry a bunch of pins in your bag and when you happen upon any sort of political activity (picketers, rallies, etc.) you set to work. Of course you don't have to wait for an event, but in such an atmosphere you'll find half the work is done for you. The patriotic folks are already wound up and ready to take action. And what better way for an American to take action than to buy something?

Downsides

• If you happen to be toting the pins for the party your customer opposes, you may well find yourself snubbed, heckled, or worse.

• You'll have a much harder time selling when it's not a major election year. Local and state elections just don't inspire the same consumer frenzy.

Sites to Check Out

• **www.gop.com**—Republican National Committee. Under the "VOLUNTEER" tag, look for "GOP STUFF."

• **www.democrats.org**—The Democratic Party. Look for "Distribution Materials."

80. Sperm Donor

What You Do: At the first consultation you will be looked at, questioned, and generally sized up to see if you're the kind of "father" material they are looking for (see "What You Need" below). If you pass this initial test, you will return to the clinic to make your first sample donation, via masturbation. If, after careful analysis, the clinicians like what they see under the microscope (which cuts out about half to 90 percent of the applicants), you do it two more times. Then you go through a series of questionnaires and forms (about family history and such) and medical tests, and finally you sign a contract and get to work. The acceptance process can take anywhere from six weeks to six months, after which you will have to commit to a regular donation program for six months to three years—not to exceed ten children born by your sperm.

<u>What You Get:</u> $50 to $200 per specimen

<u>What It Costs:</u> Nothing

<u>What You Need:</u> You must be male, between the ages of 18 and 40, at least five-foot eleven, and of proportionate weight. You have to have a high school degree at least and probably proof of higher education. If you are rich, gorgeous, and a genius, you'll have a better chance of being accepted. Obviously you have to be totally disease-free, too.

<u>Perks</u> Ummm, I'm not going there.

<u>Downsides</u>
• The more children born by your sperm to different families, the more chance there is for incest when they grow up. Think about it—when your full-fledged daughter gets to high school she could end up falling for your half son. That's just weird.

• You have to maintain abstinence for about a week prior to giving a sample.

• The application process is pretty long and involved, and there's a really good chance you won't be accepted, which, I imagine, can be rather humbling, in addition to being a big waste of time.

<u>Sites to Check Out</u>
• **www.pinelandpress.com/faq/donor.html# sperm**—A list of sperm banks across the country.

• **www.spermcenter.com/formen.htm** gives a walk-through of the donation process.

• **www.spermbankdirectory.com/sbpurchases perm.htm**—More of your questions answered.

81. Egg Donor

<u>What You Do:</u> First you undergo an extensive series of physical and psychological tests and a family history background check. You will be given information about your rights and responsibilities and have an opportunity to ask questions before you sign forms agreeing to all the terms and conditions. Next you receive an injection to suppress your natural menstrual cycle and begin taking fertility drugs, continuing to undergo routine checkups. About five weeks after your first injection, the eggs are removed from the ovaries via a minor surgical procedure.

<u>What You Get:</u> $6,000 to $8,000

<u>What It Costs:</u> Nothing

<u>What You Need:</u> You must be a female between the ages of 21 and 35 and in good health with a clean background. There is a high demand for Jewish and Asian donors and women with particular educational, professional, or artistic accomplishments who are also attractive, smart, friendly, and everything else a couple would want their child to be.

<u>Perks</u>
• Though in most cases the recipients will never know who you are, you will always know you have given them something very special.

<u>Downsides</u> (Okay, here we go . . .)
- Potential side effects of the initial shot include hot flashes, sleep problems, soreness, fatigue, headaches, mood swings, and vision problems.

- Side effects of the fertility prescription may include fluid retention, soreness, redness, and mild bruising. It is possible to experience a condition known as "Ovarian Hyperstimulation Syndrome," or OHSS, which in severe cases leads to blood clots, kidney failure, fluid buildup in the lungs, or shock.

- There is little data on the long-term effects of egg donation because it is a relatively new procedure. Some studies have indicated that it increases the risk of ovarian cancer later in life.

- It is not easy for most women to know they have genetic offspring in the world that they will never meet.

- There are many ethical and religious considerations to take into account, as well. Some women experience feelings of guilt or a sense of loss after donating eggs.

<u>Sites to Check Out</u>
- **www.health.state.ny.us/nysdoh/infertility/ eggdonor.htm**—This is a very informative site that will answer many questions you may have on the process, risks, laws, etc.

- **www.fertilityfutures.com**—Fertility Futures International has both egg donation and surrogacy programs.

- **www.eggdonor.com** is another international egg donor program.

82. Body Part Model

What You Do: Do you have stunning ears? Lovely hands? A gorgeous neck? Cute toes? Body part models are often used for advertisements that focus on only a small part of the body (such as jewelry, shoe, shaving products, or some food ads), or as a replacement when the main model for an advertisement has a great face and figure but crooked fingers, a scar across her ankle, or is in any way deficient when zoomed in on closely. There are a couple of ways to get into body part modeling. One is to set up an appointment with a modeling agency. Alternately, you can go directly to stores you would like to model for and ask if they currently advertise. If so, find out where they get their models. If not, you might be able to convince them that using a fine model like yourself could increase their sales. Whichever route you choose, go equipped with photos of your body part of choice (preferably in poses emulating popular ads) and be sure your overall appearance is neat and professional. You may think you're only showing off your feet, but nobody likes to hire a slob—for anything, but especially not for modeling.

What You Get: From $20/hour to $1,000+ for an afternoon of shooting. Your pay will depend on whom you're modeling for, how much experience you have, and how extraordinary your feet/hands/ears/neck/belly button/teeth really are.

What It Costs: Nothing. Don't sign up with an agency that charges you for professional photographs. You shouldn't have to pay anything to get representation, and you can have a friend take some good photos for free. If an agency honestly likes you, they'll know they can make money off you by getting you work and taking a percentage of your earnings—they won't need to scam you into paying for services you don't need.

<u>What You Need:</u> Obviously, whatever part of the body you're trying to market has to be exceptionally attractive. You don't have to be all-around gorgeous like many other sorts of models, but it never hurts. If an agency is choosing between two sets of beautiful hands and one set is attached to a beautiful body with a beautiful face and the other is not, chances are the first one will get the gig.

<u>Perks</u>
• Start by modeling a toe ring and you might end up a movie star. Actress Elisha Cuthbert (*The Girl Next Door*, *House of Wax*) began her career at a young age as a foot model in the late 1980s.

<u>Downsides</u>
• Foot models be warned—there's a much higher demand for foot fetish party participants than for classy designer heels models. So if you're into sucking chocolate off your toes for someone else's entertainment, great, but if not, be sure you know what you're signing up for. There have got to be folks out there with hand or belly button fetishes, too, but I haven't run into any yet—nevertheless, it's always good to do a little research before you show up for a shoot.

<u>Sites to Check Out</u>
• **www.lindarose.com/art-handmodel.asp**—Some wisdom for aspiring hand models.

• **www.fashiongates.com** includes a section of international listings for parts models.

• **www.bodypm.com**—To get ideas for good poses and to see what the competition is like, give this site a visit.

83. Hair Sales

What You Do: Chop off at least twelve inches of hair and sell it or auction it off.

What You Get: Around $8 per ounce, although hair at auctions often goes for more than $1,000 a foot.

What It Costs: You can get a pair of scissors for a few dollars, or go to your local salon.

What You Need: You should have at least a foot of hair to sell, and you will get the best price if it has not been bleached or otherwise damaged. Of course long, luscious, beautiful locks will be worth the most.

Perks
• If you're going to cut it anyway, you might as well make some money while you're at it.

Downsides
• You have to be careful when selling/auctioning off hair online. Unfortunately, there's a high likelihood that you will receive perverted e-mails from folks looking for more than a nice wig. Don't agree to let a buyer cut your hair, and make it clear that you will not be including a video of the cutting process (which some buyers would then turn around and sell online at disreputable sites for exorbitant prices). Also be sure that you receive the check and have the money in the bank before you ship the hair.

• It takes a long time to grow back.

<u>Sites to Check Out</u>
- Place an add at **www.hairwork.com/bidhere .htm** for $20 to begin the auctioning process.

- **www.cindycut.com/buyhair.htm** will buy certain hair—if you send them twelve inches or more, they'll either send you a check or return it to you if they can't use it.

- **www.europeanhumanhair.com** is another buyer whom you can contact via their Web site for details.

TIPS

- Hair should be clean, dry, and bundled in a pony tail or braid before being placed in a plastic bag and shipped in a padded envelope.
- Layered hair can be separated into several ponytails of different lengths and sold individually.
- If you have curly hair, pull it straight before measuring. This is a legitimate practice and expected by experienced buyers, though you can make a note of it in your ad if you feel so inclined.
- When having pictures taken of your hair for an ad (assuming you place an ad before you cut it), don't only be concerned about the glossiness of your locks. Stand up straight and wear attractive clothing. If you present an overall positive image, potential buyers will want to look like you, and having your hair is a good place to start.

84. Plasma Sales

<u>What You Do:</u> Check in the yellow pages or at a local college for the nearest plasma collection center or blood bank (there are more than 400 for-profit plasma collection centers in the United

States). Make an appointment, and be sure to eat something about two hours before you go. Allow three hours for your first appointment so that they can do a thorough medical history check on you—subsequent visits will be much shorter. Once you're determined to have good blood (no diseases, etc.) you can lie back and let it flow. This part of the process takes half an hour to an hour.

<u>What You Get:</u> Up to $35/collection, and you can donate twice a week (with plasma donation, the non-plasma part of the blood is pumped back into you so that your system is not as depleted as it is after whole blood donations, which can only be made once every eight weeks).

<u>What It Costs:</u> Nothing

<u>What You Need:</u> You must be in good health, between the ages of 17 and 60, and at least 110 pounds. For a more complete list of requirements, visit **www.bloodbook.com/donr-requir.html**.

<u>Perks</u>
• The most work you'll have to do is to squeeze your hand to get the blood going.

<u>Downsides</u>
• Giving frequently can cause iron depletion and scarring.

• Folks who sell plasma may not be treated with the same kind of attention and respect that those who donate are.

Sites to Check Out
- **www.nationalplasmacenters.com** offers advice for giving/selling blood and can direct you to a collection site.

- **http://bloodbanker.com** has all sorts of related links, including blood bank sites, humor, and news.

TIPS

- Drink lots of water after each visit.

- Don't drink alcohol for 72 hours afterwards.

- Don't plan physical activity immediately following visits—though it's not as taxing as giving whole blood, you still might feel a little off.

85. Medical or Psychological Study Participant

What You Do: You aid research by being a guinea pig for scientists or doctors to test theories on. Only it's not as bad as that sounds—usually. If done through a verifiable organization, there's a very slim chance you'll be asked to do anything that hasn't already been tested to ensure it won't cause you permanent damage. You might have to swallow pills, stay awake, receive injections, respond to questions, exercise, sit around, or any number of other things. Whatever you do, you will be monitored closely, either at a facility where you might be required to stay for the length of the study, or during routine visits to the study center or lab.

<u>What You Get:</u> This depends on the length and nature of the study. I've seen a 48-hour sleep deprivation study offering $525; $1,000 for seven days for individuals with a family history of alcoholism; and $3,850 for a two week in-patient study on cardiovascular health. I once got $12 to stare at a computer screen and punch a button to test the connection between reflexes and reading ability.

<u>What It Costs:</u> Nothing

<u>What You Need:</u> Requirements will depend entirely on the study. You might have to be an obese male with a history of compulsive gambling, or a petite 22-year-old woman who never smokes, never drinks, and never sleeps around. It just depends. Many studies just want average, healthy adults. Studies on sleep issues are common, so if you have trouble sleeping, it could be your ticket to some easy cash.

<u>Perks</u>
- If the study requires you to stay at a facility, you will be provided with room and board along with a paycheck.

- You'll probably get to learn a few things in the process, about yourself, or about medicine or psychology. However, be forewarned that you may not get the results back from all the testing. You are being tested for *their* information, not for your own.

<u>Downsides</u>
- There are plenty of risks involved, even if not long-term or devastating. (This applies mostly to tests where you have to swallow pills or receive

injections or things like that.) If they were sure the medicines they were testing were 100 percent safe and effective, they wouldn't have to test them.

Sites to Check Out

• **www.clinilabs.net** is an accredited diagnostic and treatment center in Manhattan.

• **www.researchfolk.com** is another one, also in New York.

• **www.clinicaltrials.gov** has lots of useful information and links.

• **http://clinicalstudies.info.nih.gov** is also very informative.

86. Body Advertising

<u>What You Do:</u> There is a new wave of advertising in which companies pay an individual to get a tattoo of the company's logo or Web site address. The tattoos are temporary (most last about a month) and can usually be placed on the body part of your choice, as long as it's regularly visible to the public. Basically, you live your life like you normally would, and when people comment on your tattoo you talk to them about the company you're representing.

<u>What You Get:</u> Generally from $100 to $5,000, depending on the size and location of the tattoo (your forehead will make more money than your lower back). You might get lucky and earn a whole lot more—body advertising gained notoriety recently when Andrew Fischer auctioned off his forehead on eBay for $37,375.

<u>What It Costs:</u> Nothing

<u>What You Need:</u> You will be a promising candidate if you are friendly and outgoing, attractive, and you will give the tattoo a lot of exposure—for example, if you work at a popular bar or nightclub or have a reputation that will make you particularly appealing to consumers.

<u>Perks</u>
• It's easy money. You don't have to do anything you wouldn't normally do, except explain to people why the heck you have a Web site address tattooed across your forehead.

• It's temporary (although some companies are willing to pay more for a real tat). Even if you hate being a walking billboard, it'll only last a month and you never have to do it again if you don't want to.

<u>Downsides</u>
• If the writing's too small you'll have a lot of strangers poking their noses right up to your forehead trying to read what it says.

<u>Sites to Check Out</u>
• **www.leaseyourbody.com** is basically an agency for body advertisers. You enter your profile, select which body part you'd like to "lease" and how much you'll do it for, and wait for a job. Signing

up is free, but the agency will take a percentage of your earnings.

- **www.bodybillboardz.com**—You can advertise yourself on this Web site. Also check out the car, T-shirt, and pet advertising!

- **www.tatad.com** is another agency well worth looking into.

Chapter Seven

ODDEST OF
THE ODD

Category-Defying Jobs

Video Game Tester

Betta Fish Breeding
Live Mannequin
Furniture Tester
Mystery Shopper
Game Show Contestant
Movie or Television Extra
Video Game Tester
Substitute Teacher
Transcription
Club Bouncer
Organ Courier
Vacuum Dust Sorter
Carcass Collector
Collecting Cans
Sleep Director

*Here's to the crazy ones, the misfits, the rebels,
the troublemakers, the round pegs in the square holes . . .
they push the human race forward, and while some may
see them as the crazy ones, we see genius, because
the ones who are crazy enough to think that
they can change the world, are the ones who do.*

—Steve Jobs

87. Betta Fish Breeding

<u>What You Do:</u> It's best to start with at least four healthy betta fish (two male and two female), all kept in separate tanks within view of each other. After three or four days move one of the males into a breeding tank, which should hold at least five inches of water that is 80 to 82 degrees Fahrenheit. You'll want to have it decorated with a few aquatic plants—no, it's not about romantic ambience, it's more about survival skills (the female may need to hide at certain points). After a few hours, you can add the female betta, watch them try to tear each other to pieces, and by the end of the day you'll probably have a bubble nest with a bunch of fertilized eggs, as well as two exhausted, injured betta fish (which can be rehabilitated with a little T.L.C.).

<u>What You Get:</u> $150 to $200 per breeding. Betta fish go for $2.50 to $5 apiece, and you get 40 to 100 little bettas per batch (probably minus a few that become a post-mating snack).

<u>What It Costs:</u> $100 to $150 for tanks (you'll want to keep the male fish away from each other and in separate tanks from the females until they're ready to mate . . . there's a reason they're also called Siamese Fighting Fish), four fish, and fish food. You might look on **www.craigslist.com**, or at local flea markets or tag sales for used tanks. You can even use a glass vase with a wide mouth at first. Once the babies are about a half-inch long, you can put them in individual glass jars until they're ready to sell.

<u>What You Need:</u> Though pretty much anyone can breed bettas, it's a good idea to know what you're doing. Do your research.

<u>Perks</u>
• You can breed the same couple every two weeks or so, which makes for a lot of babies!

<u>Downsides</u>
• You have to keep an eye on the little fish—after about thirty weeks they will be big enough to start fighting. If you're not careful, they'll eat up half your profits, literally.

<u>Sites to Check Out</u>
• **www.aquaticcommunity.com**—There are some good articles here on bettas and breeding techniques.

• **http://care.betta-fish.com.ar**—All about betta fish care.

• **www.bettatalk.com**—More about bettas, including stories, humor, and betta sculptures for the true betta lover.

88. Live Mannequin

<u>What You Do:</u> Pose as part of a window display or at a store's entrance, sporting the shop's latest fashions. Businesses have found that live mannequins attract more attention than the traditional plastic ones, which really isn't much of a surprise—of course it's more fun to look at a beautiful model in a short skirt than a freaky inanimate object with bad hair.

<u>What You Get:</u> $25 to $100/hour

<u>What It Costs:</u> Nothing

<u>What You Need:</u> You'll have a better chance of getting a job if you're attractive. That's just the way it is, I'm afraid. However, if you've always dreamed of being part of a window display but you don't have daddy long legs and a waist that disappears when you turn sideways, don't despair. I once saw a girl in a shop window with one of those electric vibrating belts that's supposed to zap away your fat. She was not your typical model (she was, in fact, rather "fleshy" around the waist) and she was jiggling all over the place, smiling and bouncing in her sports bra and spandex, and probably making a pretty penny for it.

<u>Perks</u>
• Hang out at a mall wearing brand new clothes.

• Watching people's expressions light up and contort as they realize you're not made of plastic

<u>Downsides</u>
• Standing still as a statue wearing high heels for long periods of time—not really that fun.

Sites to Check Out
- **www.freezemodeling.com**—This site's goal is to "present our appreciation of this art, share our love for the models, and to trade stories about this and other motionless topics." It's kind of a weird site, actually, but what do you expect? It's an odd job.

89. Furniture Tester

<u>What You Do:</u> Sit in various sorts of rocking chairs, love seats, and recliners; wiggle around, rock back and forth, lean back, lean forward; assess your level of comfort; move to next chair; repeat. You may be required to test up to 200 or more pieces a day, which, according to La-Z-Boy tester Mike Pixley, can be quite a workout. He says he lost 18 pounds his first summer on the job, apparently from all the up and down and back and forth movements.

<u>What You Get:</u> $6 to $10/hour

<u>What It Costs:</u> Nothing

<u>What You Need:</u> The ideal furniture tester, according to a La-Z-Boy test lab supervisor, is 180 to 200 pounds and at least six feet tall.

Perks
• Suddenly, being a slacker before, during, or after a day on the job becomes "training," "work," or "research."

Downsides
• If you tell people you sit for a living and then complain about sore abdominal muscles (which is apparently an issue for many new testers), you're not going to get much sympathy.

Sites to Check Out
• **www.consumerreports.com**—*Consumer Reports* hires a staff to test products, including mattresses and chairs.

• **www.cartalk.com/content/read-on/1999/ 10.09.2.html**—Mike Pixley, tester for La-Z-Boy, was interviewed on *Car Talk*. You can read about it here.

90. Mystery Shopper

What You Do: Go to a shop, bank, car dealership, or restaurant, pose as a normal customer, and evaluate your shopping experience. Oftentimes you will be given a certain amount of money to spend, but other times (like at a car dealership) you will pretend you are interested in making a purchase without actually buying anything. Your goal is to gather as much information about the service, quality, and quantity of products, cleanliness of the facility, and overall atmosphere to report back to the owner of the store/restaurant/bank.

<u>What You Get:</u> Expect around $100/month in money, food, and merchandise, if you work for one company and do one assignment a week, for a total of 2 to 4 hours over the whole month. You can make more if you sign up with multiple companies.

<u>What It Costs:</u> Nothing. Don't pay a cent to sign up with a company. There are plenty of companies that don't require a fee to apply.

<u>What You Need:</u> You must be an adult and you should be observant and able to carry out the instructions provided by the company you work for. Customer service experience is helpful but not necessary, and you should live in or near an area where there are chain stores and restaurants. Regular Internet access is important, too, as it is usually via e-mail that companies recruit for assignments and receive completed reports.

<u>Perks</u>
- Flexibility. You can accept or reject a job at your discretion, and if you agree to an assignment you are usually allowed several days in which to complete it.

- Fun. What's more fun than shopping with someone else's money?

- Free stuff. You get to keep whatever you buy on assignment, as long as you don't spend more than the amount allotted you.

Downsides

- Assignments are pretty sporadic. Some people manage to make a living as a mystery shopper, but it's not easy. In order to work more than a few times a month you have to sign up with lots of companies, which means being very organized with your contacts and paperwork. You don't want to report back to the wrong company— sharing information between companies is a big taboo in the mystery shopping world!

- Generally you can't be sent to the same store more than once, which means if there are not a lot of stores in your area, you won't have a lot of work.

Sites to Check Out

- **www.idealady.com/shopping.htm**—This is a very informative site that will demystify all the elements of mystery shopping for you.

- **www.mysteryshop.org** is an international professional trade association dedicated to mystery shopping. Here you can learn about becoming certified, which can sometimes get you more work, though it is not a requirement for many companies.

- Here are some companies to sign up with: **www.mystery-shoppers.com**, **www.bmiltd.com**, and **www.iccds.com**.

91. Game Show Contestant

<u>What You Do:</u> Pick a game show you'd like to be on, make yourself familiar with its rules and the sorts of people who make it on air, and look up its Web site to find out how to apply. Some games hold open auditions, some require a fairly extensive written application followed by an audition, and others just want basic information from you because contestants are selected at random from a list of interested individuals. If you make it on, you get to play a game and, hopefully, rake in the cash!

<u>What You Get:</u> For most shows you only make money if you win—you won't get a check just for playing. However, with some games it's almost guaranteed that you'll make at least a little bit. *Wheel of Fortune*, for example, is a game where nearly all of the contestants leave with a contribution to their bank accounts, whereas if you make it up on the stage of *The Price Is Right* there's a pretty good chance you'll be climbing back down without an extra penny.

<u>What It Costs:</u> Generally nothing, unless you have to book a flight to L.A. for an interview or for filming (most game shows are held in L.A., with the notable exceptions *Who Wants to Be a Millionaire?* and *The Weakest Link*, which are filmed in New York City).

<u>What You Need:</u> This, of course, depends on what show you're going for. But besides the obvious (like you have to know a whole lot of trivia to make it on *Jeopardy!*), there are a few things almost all

game show scouts look for. One, you probably have to be over eighteen, unless it's specifically a kid's show. Two, you should be a friendly, happy, likeable person—someone that people like to watch. Keep this in mind if you make it to an audition. From the moment you walk in the door, keep a pleasant smile on your face, speak and hold yourself confidently, be a gracious loser, and let your enthusiasm shine when you win. For many game shows, the rule seems to be the bubblier the better. Also, it might be to your advantage if you're not from the area where the show is filmed, as out-of-town contestants are harder to find and thus in greater demand.

Perks

• People will always be impressed when you tell them you were on a game show, even if you lost pathetically.

• If you do win, you usually win a lot.

• It's fun! (It is a game, after all.)

Downsides

• It's *not* fun to make humiliating mistakes in front of a worldwide audience.

• The vast majority of people who try out for game shows simply don't make it.

• Winnings are taxed just like any other income.

Sites to Check Out

• **www.seeing-stars.com/ShowBiz/Tips.shtml**— Good advice for contestant wannabes.

- **www.ukgameshows.com** is a very British site with some very helpful articles, links, and other information.

- **http://gameshow.ipbhost.com** is a discussion board about game shows.

POPULAR GAME SHOWS

- *Jeopardy!*—**www.jeopardy.com**

- *The Price Is Right*—go to **www.cbs.com** and follow links to the game show's information page.

- *Who Wants to Be a Millionaire?*—**www.millionairetv .com**

- *Wheel of Fortune*—**www.wheeloffortune.com**

- *Family Feud*—**www.familyfeud.tv**

92. Movie or Television Extra

<u>What You Do:</u> Sign up with a local talent agency, or watch for advertisements in the paper for film or television companies coming to your area. Or you can just show up on site and ask really nicely for a spot—sometimes it works. At the shoot you will probably spend most of your time in the "holding room," or, if the shoot is outside, the "holding tent." When you are needed for a scene you will be herded to the correct place and told what to do. Extras are hired for large crowd scenes, such as dining halls, busy parks, or a crowded bus. Most likely you will only be a blur in the background, if that—I spent about thirteen hours on a Verizon

Wireless commercial shoot, along with about 200 other extras, and was even asked to do a walk-by cameo role, but when the ad came out you could only see about ten people total—and I wasn't one of them. However, it's possible that you will be selected to do a featured extra role where you will be more visible, or maybe even be assigned an unscripted line.

<u>What You Get:</u> Assuming you're not a SAG (Screen Actors Guild) member, you can expect $100 to $200/day (be warned that days are often long—twelve- to fifteen-hour days are not unusual—and sometimes start before dawn).

<u>What It Costs:</u> Nothing

<u>What You Need:</u> Virtually anyone can be an extra. You don't really have to act, you just have to be able to follow directions.

<u>Perks</u>
• There's usually plenty of good food provided.

• You'll have tons of extra time to hang out, which means time to meet interesting people, play cards, work on a project, or take a nap.

• You will get to see the inner workings of a set and likely be in close proximity to famous actors or actresses.

• If you end up being promoted to a featured extra role or a speaking part, you may be able to get your SAG card, which will guarantee you a lot more money, health insurance, better treatment, and more attention at your gigs (though you do have to pay union dues and may not get as many gigs, because SAG members are only allowed to do union jobs).

Downsides
- Having to arrive at the break of dawn, only to sit for hours and hours before you are asked to do anything.

- When you get work through agencies (which is the most promising way to do it), they will take about 20 percent of your earnings.

- It really stinks when you think you are signed up for a job, you arrive before the sun has even considered rousing itself, and then you get sent home because they booked too many extras by accident (unfortunately, these things happen, and there's not much you can do about it).

Sites to Check Out
- **www.soyouwanna.com/SITE/SYWS/movie-extra/movieextra.html** offers helpful advice for movie extra hopefuls.

- **www.entertainmentcareers.net** includes more advice and some job postings.

- **www.craigslist.com** often includes listings for extra positions, especially in the Los Angeles area.

LINGO

- "Blocking," in this case, is not a karate move. It's when you're told where to stand or sit for a scene.

- "Craft Service" is a table of snacks that is provided all day for extras, actors, and actresses.

- "Tafted" or "Taft-Hartleyed" means getting into the SAG union by being asked to speak a line or by filling in for a union member on three different occasions, which only happens if a union member doesn't show and they happen to pick you to take his or her place.

93. Video Game Tester

<u>What You Do:</u> Play and assess video games that are in the process of being developed. You will be looking for art glitches, logic errors, levels that are too hard or too easy, spelling mistakes, ways to "outwit" the system, etc. You will probably have to play the same game, and maybe even the same level of the same game, over and over and over, and then write thorough critiques to give back to the developer.

<u>What You Get:</u> $9 to $12/hour part time, or around $30,000/year for full time entry-level positions.

<u>What It Costs:</u> Nothing

<u>What You Need:</u> You must be an expert gamer. This may sound like a joke of a job, but you really have to know your stuff. Gaming companies won't take just anyone, and preference will be given to those who have experience with a variety of gaming systems and who can prove their skill. You must also have an eye for detail and be able to clearly describe, in oral or written form, any glitches or flubs you discover.

<u>Perks</u>
• Play games for cash!

• This is also an opportunity to get your foot in the game development world if this is a field you want to move into.

<u>Downsides</u>
• Blurry eyes and sensations that closely resemble those of a zombie.

<u>Sites to Check Out</u>
• **www.gametester.com** has a directory of employers and links to useful articles.

• **www.gamediscovery.com**—Everything gaming related, including job listings and a description of what game testers do.

TIPS

• When inquiring about game testing jobs, call them "quality assurance positions." It sounds much more professional.

• There are a bazillion sites out there that promise you big bucks for playing games, if you just sign up, for a one-time membership fee of . . . yada yada yada. Don't fall for it. Contact gaming companies directly if you want a job, or go to one of the jobs listed on the sites referenced above, but don't pay anybody—that defeats the purpose of getting a job.

94. Substitute Teaching

<u>What You Do:</u> Fill in for the regular teachers who might be sick, on vacation, or at a conference. Generally teachers will leave lesson plans for you to follow, but you can count on there being opportunities for you to improvise. For lower levels espe-

cially, you will get to dabble in a variety of subjects, from P.E. to Math to Art. You may need to be fingerprinted, too.

<u>What You Get:</u> $50 to $75/day

<u>What It Costs:</u> Nothing

<u>What You Need:</u> A high school degree (or GED); for higher levels you may need to have some college credits under your belt. You also might have to go through a short training course (3 to 10 days long), depending on the specific requirements of the school at which you are applying.

<u>Perks</u>
• Variety is the spice of life, they say. Unless you become a long-term substitute, meaning you have the same class for an extended period of time, you will be hopping from subject to subject and maybe even school to school. Even if you are long-term, I don't think any two days in a teacher's life are anywhere near the same.

• If you are considering a career in teaching, this is a great way to try it out and make some useful connections.

• Teachers always learn as much as they teach, even if it's mostly things like how to evade soaring spitballs.

<u>Downsides</u>

• The first day of teaching is the hardest, and being a sub is like having a first day every time you work. Students won't know what to expect of you, and until they figure it out (which might take the whole day), some will inevitably push your limits and get away with anything they can. Some students will be skeptical of your knowledge or abilities and others simply won't care.

• Calls for subs are generally last minute, so if you like planning ahead and sticking to a schedule, this might not be the job for you.

• You can't count on there always being thorough lesson plans waiting neatly on the desk for you. It's a good idea to go prepared with some activities, books, or educational games so you're not stuck with a roomful of bored kids all day (see the resources below). Bored kids are a teacher's nightmare. Keep them gainfully occupied and you'll avoid 90 percent of the typical classroom trials.

<u>Sites to Check Out</u>

• **www.schoolspring.com**—Search for teaching jobs by state, category (choose substitute), and grade level.

• **www.educationworld.com**—This site is incredibly extensive, with pages and pages of lesson plans, activities, articles, and a section specifically for subs.

• **www.csrnet.org/csrnet/substitute**—Here you'll find links to lesson plans and teaching tips by subject. Some of the links are outdated, but there are enough current ones to make it worth a visit.

95. Transcription

<u>What You Do:</u> Listen to recordings of focus groups, court trials, or medical reports, type what you hear in a prescribed format, and return it to the employer for their records.

<u>What You Get:</u> $10 to $20/hour. Some companies pay per assignment rather than by the hour, but it evens out to about the same amount.

<u>What It Costs:</u> Nothing. You will need some sort of audio playback system which will allow you to start and stop, rewind, and fast forward the recording (which will usually be sent to you in a file via the Internet) easily. You can purchase a system operated by a foot pedal, or you can download a simple system for free (see link below).

<u>What You Need:</u> You must be a relatively fast typist (60 words per minute or faster) and have a working knowledge of grammar. For medical transcription jobs you will need a more in-depth understanding of medical terminology and probably some experience in the field.

<u>Perks</u>
• You work on your own time, wherever you can take your computer.

<u>Downsides</u>
• You'll find your eyes getting sore from concentrating so hard (at least I did, but maybe that's just me).

<u>Sites to Check Out</u>
- **www.nch.com.au/scribe**—Free audio playback software

- **http://transcriptionist.jobs.com** has job listings.

- **www.mtjobs.com** focuses on medical transcription jobs.

96. Club Bouncer

<u>What You Do:</u> Patrol clubs, looking for underage guests or potential troublemakers. If there's a fight, it's your job to break it up. If someone tries to go where they shouldn't (like in the manager's office), it's your job to stop them. When it's time to close, it's your job to politely kick everybody out. And then there are the other little responsibilities that might not be in your job description but which you'll inevitably end up doing, like directing drunk women to the bathroom and refusing to give out your phone number (or not refusing) several times a night.

<u>What You Get:</u> $9 to $15/hour

<u>What It Costs:</u> Nothing

<u>What You Need:</u> Chances are you won't get the job unless you're male and you look like an angry football player. However, there are exceptions, and you can improve your chances by mentioning any mar-

tial arts or other self-defense training you've had. Also, you should be capable of calmly handling tense situations without letting yourself get too riled up. There has been more than one bouncer who tried to break up a fight and ended up with a physical assault or even a murder charge on his hands.

Perks
- If you like the club scene, you'll get plenty of it. You'll be staring at scads of scantily clad women all night long, and your pulse will be throbbing with the beats till dawn.

Downsides
- You're not supposed to socialize—you're pretty much bound to a "you can look but you can't touch" policy.

- You're supposed to intimidate club goers into behaving without actually using force, if possible. This means if the intimidation doesn't work, you might end up accepting a few blows without being able to throw any back. However, ideally you should be able to restrain anyone who gives you trouble and calmly boot them out of the club.

Sites to Check Out
- **www.ehow.com/how_12362_become-bouncer.html** offers some useful tips of the trade.

- **www.crimedoctor.com/nightclub_security_3.htm**—This article will give you a good idea of what employers are looking for and what you can and cannot do on the job.

- **www.mkeonline.com/story.asp?id=1394228**—Read about one former attorney's new life as a bouncer.

97. Organ Courier

<u>What You Do:</u> Transport kidneys, blood, hearts, or other organs or medical specimens. Live organs will probably be packed in a Styrofoam ice chest and may need to be rushed from one hospital to another, or from a hospital to an airport. Other organs may be used for medical testing, in which case you'd be delivering the goods to a lab.

<u>What You Get:</u> $8 to $20/hour

<u>What It Costs:</u> Nothing

<u>What You Need:</u> A license, a car (in some cases a car or van is provided), and the ability to follow directions—both where you're going and what you have to do when you get there.

<u>Perks</u>
• Every time you deliver a live kidney, you're helping to save a life.

<u>Downsides</u>
• If you make a mistake, it's a big deal. One courier loaded the Styrofoam container onto the plane, satisfied with a job well done. The next day he received a call from the waiting hospital staff—their patient was lying in the hospital bed with a catheter in his neck and anti-rejection drugs pulsing through his blood, and they hadn't

received the kidney. Later that day, the unfortunate man found the kidney in his trunk, ruined—he had shipped the wrong container. The poor patient was sewn back up, put back on the waiting list, and sent home. As for the courier, I imagine he was sent home, too.

Sites to Check Out

• **www.quickintl.com**—Here's an international courier company that specializes in medical shipments. Check out the pressroom for some intriguing courier stories.

• **www.medicalcouriers.net**—A U.S.-based medical courier service.

• **www.organtransplants.org**—Anyone who's going to be a kidney chauffeur should know at least a little about organ transplants. This site will get you up to speed.

98. Vacuum Dust Sorter

<u>What You Do:</u> Offer to take the full vacuum bags from commercial cleaners, then sift through each bag looking for treasure. You'll get some strange looks when you make your request, but the reality is that you're saving them the money for disposal. You can also ask for old rugs when they're being thrown out, and do the vacuuming yourself.

<u>What You Get:</u> It's a gamble. You might find a few coins, a diamond, or a bunch of dried up spider eggs. One California man professed to discovering over $2,000 worth of coins, precious stones, and

rings when he took a shag rug that an old theater was disposing of.

<u>What It Costs:</u> $3 for a bag of latex gloves. You don't want your bare hands in that stuff.

<u>What You Need:</u> Patience, perseverance, and absolutely no dust allergies

Perks
• Hunting for lost treasure has always held a certain thrill. Remember when you used to dig holes way down deep in the sandbox? It's basically the same concept: a bunch of dirt and the potential to strike it rich. The gold miners had a thing for it, too.

Downsides
• Whip out those four leaf clovers, because otherwise it's going to take a lot of bags of dirt before you find the one that'll make you wealthy.

Sites to Check Out
• **www.discountvacuums.com**—If you don't have a good vacuum, you can find one at a reasonable price here.

TIPS

• Try wearing a mask if the dust gets to your lungs.

• Using a fine sifter, or a screen stapled between a couple of dowels, is helpful.

• It's best to set up outside on a day that's not too windy, or in a garage or cellar, unless you want to spend several hours a day vacuuming your own house.

99. Carcass Collector

<u>What You Do:</u> Go to your town or county's road committee or highway department and tell them you'll collect and dispose of road kill on a pay-per-animal basis. If they say "okay," you've got a job.

<u>What You Get:</u> This will vary, but one Michigan man says he got $25 per dead deer, which is a reasonable amount to expect. You'll have to work out a pay scale based on difficulty of removal. For example, maybe squirrels, rabbits, and raccoons would be $5 apiece, and skunks $10 (in case there's lingering odor).

<u>What It Costs:</u> You're going to want a pickup truck, or something to carry the carcasses away with. If you don't already have one, don't buy one just for this job, unless it really appeals to you for some reason, in which case there might be something wrong with you. If, however, you're looking for a pickup truck anyway, and you think this might be a useful side business to help pay for it, you can probably find an older used truck for a few thousand dollars. You'll also want gloves and a shovel (total $15).

<u>What You Need:</u> A strong stomach and strong arms—deer are often seventy pounds or so, and moose—well, you'll need to call a hefty friend if you find a moose.

<u>Perks</u>
• If you have a hunting lodge, you might be able to make some nice additions to the walls.

Downsides
• Sometimes it's hard to tell if an animal is really dead when you look at it, and if it's not it could still bite you. My uncle once had a cat bite him as it was dying. He had to go to a doctor to have the cat removed from his arm because it set into rigor mortis before releasing its grip.

Sites to Check Out
• **www.clemson.edu/camm/Camm_p/Ch8/pch8 _03.pdf**—Several ways to safely and legally dispose of dead animals.

• **www.fhwa.dot.gov/webstate.htm** has links to departments of transportation for every state.

• **www.fhwa.dot.gov/webtrans.htm** includes more highway-related links.

100. Collecting Cans

What You Do: Collect soda cans or plastic bottles and turn them into recycling centers for money. The key is to go to the right places—carnivals, fairs, and festivals are ideal. If there's an entrance fee so steep it will more than wipe out your earnings, hang around just outside the gate.

What You Get: 4 to 15 cents per item. This doesn't sound like much, but some Michigan folks reportedly made over $100 a day collecting cans at a local festival. When I was a kid, there was a demolition derby race that took place in a big field in the center of town. When the crowds dispersed at the end of the morning we ran around with bags and collected a treasure trove of sticky Pepsi and Slice cans. Maybe we didn't get rich, but it was enough to get us pretty excited at the time. Even as an adult, there have been times when an extra five bucks for the highway toll and a deli egg sandwich has made me believe in the goodness of life again.

<u>What It Costs:</u> Nothing

<u>What You Need:</u> The only thing that will disqualify you for this job is if you think you're overqualified. In other words, if you're too good to pick up other people's trash, don't bother with this one (but let me tell you, you're missing out on some easy money!).

<u>Perks</u>
• You're also helping the environment and beautifying your neighborhood.

<u>Downsides</u>
• People will probably either think you're a bum or a tree-hugger.

• You know you've hit a low point when you start wishing more people would litter.

<u>Sites to Check Out</u>
• **www.bottlebill.org**—Find out which states have bottle and can deposits and how much you can get.

101. Sleep Director

<u>What You Do:</u> Sleep around. No, "Sleep Director" is not a euphemism for "prostitute," but it does involve sleeping in a different bed every night. Early in 2006, Travelodge in the U.K. hired Wayne Munnelly (aka the "Sleep Czar") to test the hotel chain's 25,000 beds. His first priority is to test the tension of the mattress and the springiness of the pillows, but his responsibilities don't end there. He also must consider the lighting and décor, evaluate the soundproofing between rooms, and taste-test the complimentary coffee and tea. It's a rough job, but somebody's got to do it.

<u>What You Get:</u> The Sleep Czar makes the equivalent of over $100,000 a year. Not too many American chains have started hiring sleep directors yet, but with the right marketing techniques I'm sure there's plenty of opportunity out there.

<u>What It Costs:</u> Nothing

<u>What You Need:</u> In order to market yourself as a potential sleep director, you should be able to demonstrate knowledge and/or experience in at least a few of the following fields: interior design (including feng shui), the hotel/resort industry, customer service (you won't be dealing with customers, but you should know how they want to be treated), and what factors generally contribute to a good night's sleep.

Perks
• What, getting paid to travel around and sleep in hotels isn't enough?

Downsides
• Ironically, the job has the potential to be exhausting. No matter how comfy the mattress, sleeping in a different bed every night isn't conducive to solid sleep patterns.

Sites to Check Out
• **http://sleepfoundation.org/**—Brush up on your sleep facts before you apply. The National Sleep Foundation has all sorts of information you can use to make a good impression at the interview.

• **www.viamagazine.com/top_stories/articles/ sleep03.asp**—This article gives some insight into what makes some hotel rooms more sleep-conducive than others.

• **http://travel.timesonline.co.uk/article/0,,17471-1454575,00.html**—Give this article a read, too—it's similar to the last one, but with some different tips.

*Always you have been told that work
is a curse and labor a misfortune.
But I say to you that when you work you
fulfill a part of earth's furthest dream,
assigned to you when that dream was born,
And in keeping yourself with labor
you are in truth loving life,
And to love life through labor is to be
intimate with life's inmost secret.*

—Kahlil Gibran

ABIGAIL R. GEHRING grew up in Wilmington, Vermont. Her first dream was to be a duck when she grew up. When that didn't work out she decided to become a writer. She has held twenty-four of the jobs listed in this book, working in locations including Hawaii, England, and Manhattan. Currently she is an editor and freelance writer in New York and resides in Edgewater, New Jersey. Visit her blog at www.myoddjobs.blogspot.com.